# CREATIVE GIFTS

## QUICK & EASY PROJECTS

CREATIVE
HOME
ARTS
—CLUB—

Minnetonka, Minnesota

# CREATIVE GIFTS
## QUICK & EASY PROJECTS

Copyright © 2004 Creative Home Arts Club

Published by North American Membership Group under license from International Masters Publishers, Inc.

**Tom Carpenter**
Creative Director

**Heather Koshiol**
Managing Editor

**Michele Stockham**
Senior Book Development Coordinator

**Gina Germ**
Book Design & Production

**Laura Holle**
Assistant Book Development Coordinator

1 2 3 4 5 / 06 05 04 03

ISBN 1-58159-206-X

**Creative Home Arts Club**
12301 Whitewater Drive
Minnetonka, MN 55343
www.creativehomeartsclub.com

# CONTENTS

# INTRODUCTION

## Welcome to
## CREATIVE GIFTS

### Your guide to
### QUICK & EASY PROJECTS

Gifts you make with your own two hands always carry more meaning. When you take time and spend energy to make something special for someone special, the gesture is even more appreciated. Plus, there seems to be a lot more excitement and satisfaction in doing the giving when you also do the creating.

That's why we put together *Creative Gifts* for you! These *Quick & Easy Projects* bring you both ideas and instructions on page after page of gift items you can make for occasions—and recipients—of all kinds!

You'll start with a beautiful photograph of the finished creation. Then, of course, you need to know what materials and tools to gather. Detailed lists support you here. And rest assured, the "ingredients" you need are not difficult to find, and the tools required are probably in your craft bag, box, drawers or cabinet already.

Then, in keeping with our Club philosophy, you see how to create the project step-by-step. These clear and instructive photos remove the guesswork from the process. You still have plenty of room for creativity ... the pictures just guarantee your crafting (and gift-giving) success!

Finally, don't forget about yourself. There's nothing wrong with creating some of these items for your own enjoyment. We're willing to bet you deserve the treat! Or, maybe you'll see a craft idea, accent or accessory that would look great in your home. That's another way to reward yourself with something special.

So start putting your gift list together for the upcoming year, put yourself on your list too, and get ready to unleash your crafting energy. Quick and easy *Creative Gifts* await you!

CREATIVE
HOME
ARTS
—CLUB—

# GIFTS FOR
# HOLIDAYS &
# CELEBRATIONS

*A year is full of reasons to get together and celebrate, and packed with occasions for which gift-giving is appropriate. Why not gear the gift to the day? That's what these ideas are all about. From tree skirts for Christmas to themed windsocks, and from decorative candles to luminarias, table accessories, easy-sew napkins and more, here are ideas and instructions for making holidays and celebrations even more special.*

# FESTIVE LUMINARIAS

*Add sparkle to special occasions with easy-to-make luminaria gifts.*

## BEFORE YOU BEGIN

*Traditional in the American Southwest, glowing luminarias make simple yet stunning holiday decorations.*

### Luminaria Designs

**Enlarge the luminaria cut-out design** (left) on a photocopier to desired size. This will serve as your template.

**If you plan to use the** template for more than three or four bags, trace the enlarged design onto a sheet of acetate for durability.

**Choose luminaria** designs that feature distinctive cutouts and easy-to-follow lines; avoid patterns with shapes that intersect.

**Purchased stencils,** available in a variety of retail stores, can also be transferred to luminarias.

### Making the Bag

**Enlarge the bag template** (below) to desired size. Using a pencil and carbon paper, transfer it to the wrong side of an 11- by 17-inch sheet of decorative paper and cut out. Be sure to transfer all the folding lines as well. Heavy-weight papers are ideal, as are rice paper and gift wrap.

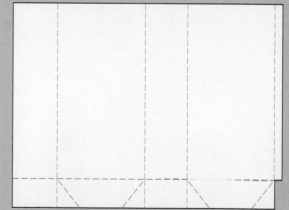

# MAKING A LUMINARIA

**1** Lay the cut-out paper bag (Before you Begin) wrong side up on a mat. Position the carbon paper over one wide side of the bag; secure with tape. Lay the template (Before you Begin) face-down on the carbon; trace.

**2** Remove the carbon and template. Using a craft knife, carefully cut around the flower and bee design. Avoid joining any cut edges together. For the scalloped edge, cut semicircles around the top of the bag.

**3** With a hole punch, punch decorative holes in the center of each scallop along the edge of the bag. Keep the bag as flat as possible to prevent the cut-out design from being torn or damaged.

**4** Referring to the template, use your fingers to crease the bag along the bottom fold-line. Continue folding the bag along the foldlines, making diagonals as needed. Crease along all foldlines.

**5** Apply craft glue along the side flap. Glue the side flap to the long edge; let dry. Remove excess glue with a damp cloth. Glue the bottom flaps of the bag together, folding and overlapping as needed to create the bag.

**6** To illuminate the luminaria, fill the bag with 1½ inches of sand and gently shake until it is level. Set one to three small tea candles in the sand. Place the bag on a tray in order to transport it safely to the display area. Light the candle with a long matchstick.

# CHRISTMAS TREE SKIRT

*Adorn the base of your tree with a simple-to-sew tree skirt ... or give it to someone special.*

## YOU WILL NEED
☐ 70-INCH TABLECLOTH
☐ 6¾ YARDS SHIRRING TAPE
☐ THREAD
☐ RIBBON
☐ SEWING MACHINE
☐ IRONING BOARD & IRON
☐ SCISSORS & PINS
☐ GOLD ORNAMENTS OR TASSLES (OPTIONAL)

## BEFORE YOU BEGIN

*Use a holiday tablecloth to create a skirt that adds a fabulous finishing touch to your tree. Select a round cloth and most of the work is already done!*

### Selecting the Fabric

• Tablecloths with stain-resistant finishes are natural for this project as they will stand up well to spilled water, dripping sap and pine needles.

• If the tree skirt fabric is lightweight, consider lining it. Sew the lining in place instead of making hems. Do this before stitching shirring tape in place.

### Cutting a Perfect Circle

To use a square tablecloth, or fabric pieced to a 70-inch square:

• Fold fabric square in half and then half again to find center point. Pin layers to prevent fabric shifting (below).

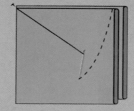

• Tie one end of string to pencil. Tack free end of string to center point of fabric so the string length equals desired radius of circle.

• Mark curved cutting line by moving pencil from corner to corner. Repeat for small inner circle, reducing the string to a 2-inch radius.

• Carefully cut at marked lines, through all fabric layers.

### Placing Shirring Tape

**Refold cut circle** to locate eight equally spaced points around circumference of circle; mark with pins. Cut eight 30-inch strips of shirring tape. Press bottom edge to wrong side. Pin shirring tapes to markings with folded edges of tapes at outer circle edges.

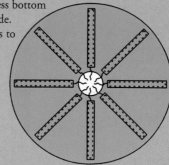

# SEWING THE TREE SKIRT

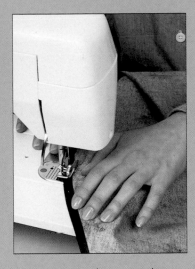

**HANDY HINTS**

For a decorative touch, bind raw edges of outer and inner circles with colorful bias tape instead of hemming.

1 Cut outer and inner circles from 70-inch tablecloth. To hem outer edge, fold edge under ½ inch to wrong side; press. Fold under ½ inch again; press and stitch close to inner fold. Repeat for smaller inner edge.

2 Refer to Before you Begin for planning and placement of shirring tape. With wrong sides together, sew tape close to long edges and across outer end of each. Leave inner end of tape unstitched.

3 To make skirt opening, mark a line from outer edge to inner edge equidistant from any two tapes; cut along line. Fold under cut edge ¼ inch again; press. Stitch close to inner fold. Do this for both cut edges.

**TAKE NOTE**

To prevent staining, apply a light coating of spray-on fabric protector to the tree skirt. The stain-resistant spray will help protect against soil, water and oil spots.

5 For decorative accent, hand stitch gold ornaments or tassels to bottom edge of tree skirt at each shirring tape. Leave a thread loop long enough for ornament to dangle from edge of skirt. Tack lengths of ribbon onto each side of opening in three places so that the tree skirt can be tied closed once it is positioned under the tree.

4 Gently pull cord of each shirring tape until excess cord measures 12 inches. Trim away excess cord; tack end to shirring tape to secure. Adjust gathers evenly. Finish inner edge of skirt by stitching a ½-inch double hem.

# DECORATIVE GLASSWARE FOR SPECIAL OCCASIONS

*Any holiday table will sparkle with the gift of this festive painted glassware.*

## BEFORE YOU BEGIN

*Gold-painted designs add instant pizzazz to almost any glassware. Trace over the provided template or any copied design for a unique look that's easy to achieve.*

### Preparing the Glass

**Remove all labels** from the glassware by soaking it in warm, soapy water. Use corn or olive oil to remove any residual glue; resoak. Give the glassware a rinsing with a half-water, half-white vinegar mixture to remove any oils and give the glassware more sparkle.

**This type of decoration** is best suited for glassware that is used infrequently. The paint will not withstand repeated washings with hot water and detergent. Acrylic enamel paints will be "wash-safe" once they are baked; follow the manufacturer's instructions.

**Trace this design** (below) onto tracing paper, then transfer the tracing to the white paper pattern. Enlarge the design on a photocopier for larger glass items, if desired.

**Don't limit yourself** to using one color for a design. Paint pens are available in a large variety of colors and metallics and can be used to draw on many smooth surfaces.

### Safety First

When using the oil-based paint pens, take care when painting glassware that will come in contact with food.
• Keep painted designs away from any areas that will be touched by food or the mouth.

• Paint the underside of plates and outside of drinking glasses—make sure to keep the designs well below "mouth level," about 1 to 2 inches from the rim.

# DECORATING GLASSWARE

## HANDY HINTS

**Paint pens** come in broad-, medium- and fine-point sizes. An opaque, oil-based paint marker with a medium tip works best for this job.

## OOPS

**If your design smudges,** wipe off immediately with a damp cloth. If the smudge has dried, carefully scrape it off with a craft knife.

1 Use gold paint pen to draw the design onto a piece of white paper to use as a pattern. Make sure the paper will fit easily inside the glass objects that are to be painted. Let paint dry before using the pattern.

2 Tape paper pattern inside wine glass, making sure top of design is more than 1 inch from lip of glass. Use gold paint pen to trace design onto outside of glass, using design on paper as a guide. Let paint dry.

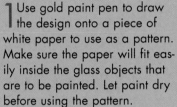

3 Tape paper pattern facedown on top side of glass plate. Paint design onto underside of plate. Be careful not to smudge paint as you move around rim. Leave plate to dry upside down.

4 Tape paper pattern inside glass vase. Paint design on outside of vase. When one part of vase has been painted, move paper pattern to adjacent area and continue painting until whole vase is covered with design. Work from bottom to top of vase.

# GIFT-LADEN WREATHS

*Create personalized wreaths laden with gifts your friends will enjoy.*

## BEFORE YOU BEGIN

*For a beautiful wreath that will be a long-lasting pleasure, choose an appropriate base and attach all the gift items securely.*

### Choosing a Base

The base must be strong enough to hold the gifts after the wreath is hung.

• Grapevine wreaths can hold the weight of most small gifts.

• Florist's foam wreath bases are suitable for lightweight decorations. There are two kinds: use absorbent bases for fresh flowers; use non-absorbent bases with dried materials.

• Straw bases are made of dried grasses compressed into a wreath shape and bound with nylon string. They can hold moderately heavy decorations, which can be easily attached with florist's picks.

• Wire wreath bases are found in many sizes and gauges, making them suitable for any weight decoration. Cover them with sphagnum moss or hay for an attractive, rustic wreath.

### How to Attach Decorations

**Grapevine Wreath:**
Hot glue or fine-gauge florist's wire.

**Dry Foam Wreath:**
U-shaped florist's picks or hot glue if covering is dense.

**Straw Wreath:**
Florist's picks, fine-gauge florist's wire or hot glue.

**Wire Wreath:**
Florist's wire or hot glue.

# MAKING THE WREATH

1 Pull handfuls of moss from bunch and position them on wreath base, binding every 4 inches with florist's wire. Pull wire tight to bury in moss. Cover base completely. Cut wire and twist ends together at back of wreath.

2 Make or purchase a garland of decorative vegetables. Use florist's wire at each end to attach garland to bottom half of wreath. Use hot glue to hold vegetables in place. Hide string with other decorations.

3 Add kitchen utensils to wreath. Thread florist's wire through holes in utensils, then wire them to wreath. Wire several utensils together for interesting composition and a balanced display.

4 Hot-glue assorted kitchen-related items to wreath. Cookie cutters, herb sachets, garlic cloves and nuts make pretty decorations. Make sure placement is well balanced.

5 Wire together small bunches of barley and assorted colors of dried flowers. Hot-glue mixed bunches to wreath to fill in any gaps left after all novelties have been attached.

6 Make a generous, three-loop bow of ribbon in colors that complement the rest of the wreath. Hot-glue in place near top of wreath. Manipulate bow to fill area and balance composition.

# HOLIDAY WINDSOCKS

*Help someone celebrate any special event with a gift of a colorful, easy-to-sew windsock.*

### YOU WILL NEED

- ❑ NYLON FABRIC
- ❑ THREAD
- ❑ SCISSORS & PINS
- ❑ RULER & PENCIL
- ❑ SEWING MACHINE & IRON
- ❑ 2 YARDS NYLON CORD
- ❑ WIRE & WIRE CUTTER
- ❑ 2 YARDS IRON-ON FUSIBLE WEB
- ❑ THREE ½-INCH PLASTIC RINGS
- ❑ TRACING PAPER

## BEFORE YOU BEGIN

*Ripstop nylon, which is often coated with a water-resistant finish, makes for a durable and attractive windsock.*

### Cutting the Fabric

Purchase 1 yard each of red, white and royal blue nylon.
• From white: Cut cylinder piece 16 by 25 inches.
• From blue: Cut band piece 4½ by 25 inches.

• From red: Cut six stripes 2 by 16 inches. Cut two 16-inch-diameter circles.
• Cut four streamers from each color of fabric 2½ by 36 inches each.

### Preparing the Brim

**To mark a circle,** tie an 8-inch piece of string to a pencil. Secure free end of string to center of fabric square. Use pencil to draw circle, keeping string taut. Mark and cut out two 16-inch-diameter circles. In the middle of each 16-inch circle, mark and cut away a 6½-inch circle. Brim pieces will be stitched together in Step 5.

### Using the Star Template

**Enlarge this star template** if desired, and trace it onto tracing paper. Copy it onto paper side of fusible web. Fuse stars onto white fabric and cut out.

# Sewing a Windsock

1 Mark ½-inch seam allowance on short ends of white cylinder piece. For red stripe placement, continue marking across width of piece every 2 inches.

2 Fuse 2- by 16-inch strips of fusible web to red stripes. Then fuse first stripe along first marking on cylinder. Continue fusing every 2 inches. With sewing machine, zigzag stitch along edges of stripes.

3 Center stars on blue band beginning ½ inch from short end; stars will almost touch. Fuse in place. Zigzag around stars. Then fuse web to wrong side of band.

### HANDY HINTS

To prevent fabric fraying, iron fusible web to back of fabric's back before cutting pieces. A liquid seam sealant also helps prevent fraying at seam allowances.

### TAKE NOTE

A cup hook is one way to hang a windsock from a house. Tie together nylon cords at top of windsock and hang from knot on cup hook.

4 Fuse blue band to bottom of cylinder with lower edges even. Zigzag along top edge of band. With right sides together, stitch long edges to form tube.

5 Stitch outer edge of red brim, leaving 1½ inches open. Clip seam allowance. Turn right side out; press. Stitch ⅜ inch from outer edge; staystitch ½ inch from inner edge.

6 Pin brim to right side of cylinder bottom. Stitch, easing to fit. To make streamers, fold edges under ¼ inch; stitch along long sides and one short end.

7 Right sides facing, stitch raw ends of streamers to inside brim edge; alternate colors. Press seam allowance to inside; stitch ¼ inch from seam, through allowances.

8 Cut wire to fit around outer edge of brim. Feed wire into opening (topstitching casing formed in Step 5). Overlap ends of wire. Stitch opening closed.

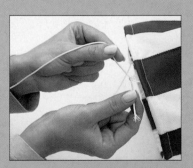

9 Fold top of cylinder under 1 inch. Stitch ½ inch from fold, leaving a 1½-inch opening. Cut wire to fit around top; insert. Sew opening closed. Tack plastic rings inside casing every 5 inches. Tie an 18-inch piece of nylon cording to each ring.

# DECORATIVE HOLIDAY CANDLES

*Transform plain candles into festive holiday decorations to give away or to decorate with.*

## BEFORE YOU BEGIN

*Candles make great decorative accents, and it couldn't be easier to dress them up. Look for all kinds of trimmings to pin or glue into place.*

### Planning the Design

**Plan the design** on paper first. Decide on the trim designs you want to use and where you want to position them, then use the pattern as an application guide.

**Studs are particularly** easy to use because they are already pronged for application. Simply push the prongs straight into the candle.

**Ribbons, gemstones**, beads and sequins can be glued with regular glue or with a drip of hot wax. Decorative craft pins may also be used to hold the trims to the candle surface.

**Use small studs** to create multiple rows to circle the candle. To keep the studs even, mark the center line of each grouping by indenting the wax with a knife.

**Combine stars and studs** for an informal yet festive candle.

**Pearl beads** with a hole for pins are also easy to apply and are more formal in appearance. They work well with a novelty ribbon at the base of the candle. You can also create a ribbon look with strips of wax appliqué.

### Star Template

Using a template makes it extremely simple to cut out wax stars to decorate the candles.
- To make a template, draw the star onto thin cardboard. Cut out and use the frame to outline the shape on the wax.

# DECORATING THE CANDLES

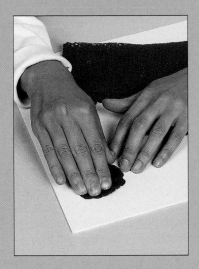

**HANDY HINTS**

To create a unique design, cut beeswax sheets into strips and then braid the strips. Attach the braid around the candle.

**OOPS**

If a candle becomes soiled, rub it with a nylon stocking to clean and restore luster.

1 Beeswax sheeting is available at craft stores and candle stores. Break off a small piece of wax from the sheet and use your fingers to softly knead and flatten it to a 1/8-inch thickness on the work surface.

2 Make a star template out of thin cardboard or stencil film (Before you Begin). Place the template on top of the flattened piece of wax. Use a craft knife to cut out as many stars as required.

3 Randomly position the stars around the candle, fixing each one in place with a small gold stud. Depending on the look you want, you can also use pins or drops of melted wax to hold the appliqués in place.

4 Decorate a shorter, wider candle with gold stars and tiny red beads all around the base. Push small gold pins through the beads and the holes in the stars to hold them all in place on the candle.

5 For the largest candle, use precut gold stars or cut your own using gold foil and star template. Position the stars randomly around the candle, using a gold stud or pin at each point to prevent curling. Combine decorative accents to make an exciting collection.

# RIBBON-COVERED GIFT BOXES

*Ribbon-covered boxes will become as treasured as the gifts they hold.*

## BEFORE YOU BEGIN

*Determining the yardage of ribbon required in advance eliminates excess ribbon and saves you time during the weaving process.*

### Determining Ribbon Lengths

**Ribbons are sold** by the yard (or meter) or in prepackaged lengths. They are available in the widths shown in the chart (there are no numbers available for the ribbon sizes marked * in the chart).

**Select a ribbon** with a width that fits evenly across the top of the box both in length and width.

**If you are using** different colors or widths of ribbon, evenly divide the total length of ribbon required between the colors and/or widths.

| Metric Ribbon Conversion Chart | | |
|---|---|---|
| Number | Inches | Millimeters |
| * | 1/16 | 1.5 |
| * | 1/8 | 3 |
| * | 3/16 | 5 |
| No. 1 | 1/4 | 7 |
| No. 1½ | 3/8 | 7 |
| No. 2 | 1/2 | 12 |
| No. 3 | 5/8 | 15 |
| No. 5 | 7/8 | 23 |
| No. 9 | 1½ | 39 |
| No. 16 | 2¼ | 56 |
| No. 40 | 3 | 77 |

### Measuring the Box

Once you have selected the ribbon, use the following method to determine the ribbon yardage that you will need:

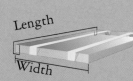

• Lengthwise ribbon: Measure box top lengthwise from inside one side to inside opposite side. Measure width of box top only (not sides). Divide width of top by width of ribbon; multiply by lengthwise measurement.
• Widthwise ribbon: Repeat procedure, substituting width for length and length for width.
• Finishing ribbon: Measure around all four sides of lid twice.
• Total yardage: Add the results of the above measurements. Purchase extra to cover errors.

### Which Ribbon

Almost any ribbon is suitable for weaving. However, avoid ribbon with a wire edge.
• Grosgrain ribbon is crisp and stable with a visible crosswise rib.
• Satin ribbon is soft and supple with an attractive, shiny surface.
• Jacquard ribbon features woven patterns, such as tapestries, florals and geometrics.
• Elegant taffeta is a very crisp and decorative type of ribbon.

# WEAVING A RIBBON BOX LID

**HANDY HINTS**

**Sturdy cardboard** boxes with lids that fit over the outside of the box are ideal for covering with ribbon. Flimsy boxes tend to lose their shape during the weaving process.

**TAKE NOTE**

**The ribbon** should lie smoothly across the box top. Do not pull it too tight or leave it too loose. The ribbons should touch but not overlap each other.

1 Paint body of box to match ribbon. When dry, sponge box with a contrasting paint color: wet sponge, wring out, then dip into paint. Dab all over sides and bottom of box.

2 Starting with lengthwise strips, hot-glue one end of ribbon inside box top. Wrap around top of box and glue other end to other side of box top. Repeat until top is covered.

4 Glue a strip of ribbon around inside and outside edges of box top to cover ends of woven ribbons. Add a ribbon loop to lid front to help open box. Embellish with a matching button.

3 Cut ribbons to desired width (Before you Begin). Hot-glue end of one ribbon inside box top; weave under then over lengthwise ribbons; pull flat, then glue in place at other end. Continue weaving, alternating over/under pattern, until box top is completely covered. Trim ribbon ends evenly inside box.

# DECORATIVE HOLIDAY DOOR TOPPER

*Give these happy snowmen and handsome pine trees to help someone greet the winter season in style.*

## YOU WILL NEED

- ❑ FOAM CORE & OAKTAG
- ❑ TISSUE PAPER
- ❑ BAMBOO SKEWERS
- ❑ WAGON WHEEL PASTA
- ❑ CRAFT GLUE
- ❑ GLUE GUN & GLUE STICKS
- ❑ ACRYLIC PAINTS
- ❑ CRAFT KNIFE
- ❑ GLOSS MEDIUM
- ❑ SCISSORS & RULER
- ❑ CLEAR ACETATE
- ❑ TRACING PAPER
- ❑ PEPPERCORNS
- ❑ DOUBLE-SIDED TAPE

## BEFORE YOU BEGIN

*Cut from foam core, this door topper is lightweight and fun. It is so easy to make that you can create a different design for each holiday.*

### Taking Measurements

Measure the door width. This door topper is 36 inches wide and 6 inches high, but adjust it based on your door size and ceiling height.

• On oaktag, draw a half-circle with a 30-inch radius.

• Measure up the half-circle, marking the points at which the arc is 36 inches wide. Draw a line connecting the points and cut out the arc for the arc template.

• When you have finalized a full-sized pattern, lay clear acetate over the tracing paper. With a ruler, carefully copy the design onto the acetate.

• Trace the template on foam core. With a craft knife or jeweler's saw, cut out the arc shape.

• Cut a foam core base 36 by 2 inches. The base will be glued to the arc at a 90-degree angle along the long edge.

### Preparing the Design

**Make templates** of the tree (right) and snowman (below) in varying sizes. Trace four snowmen onto foam core and cut them out with a craft knife, keeping the edges smooth and even. Trace five trees directly onto the foam core arc after the tissue paper has dried.

**Soften wago**n wheel pasta shapes in boiling water for two minutes, or soak them in very hot tap water for five minutes. Cut each wheel in half. Dip each cut piece of pasta into a thinned gloss medium to prevent cracking while handling. Spray paint them after the pasta is cooled.

# MAKING A DOOR TOPPER

### HANDY HINTS

**Try using** a jeweler's saw to cut the foam core. It is easily found at a craft supply store and is an inexpensive but indispensable tool.

**Paint both sides** of the foam core to prevent warping.

1 Thin craft glue with water and, working in one section at a time, apply torn, crinkled, white tissue paper over arc (Before you Begin). Be sure to cover all sides. Smooth tissue to remove any air bubbles.

2 Using two coats, paint topper with red paint and base with blue. Using template (Before you Begin), trace trees onto topper. Fill in trees with two coats of green paint. Paint white snowflakes around trees.

3 Cover snowmen (Before you Begin) with craft glue; apply torn tissue bits to front. Once dry, paint white. Using craft knife, cut bamboo skewers into small pieces for noses and arms.

### TAKE NOTE

**Use fabric scraps** from other projects instead of tissue to make scarves and hats for the snow family on the door topper.

4 Mold snowmen's hats, scarves, gloves and noses from tissue soaked in craft glue. Attach gloves and noses to cut skewers; glue painted noses to faces and paint facial details. Glue on peppercorns for coal buttons.

5 Paint arms and hats and attach to snowmen. Attach base (Before you Begin). Glue long skewers to backs of snowmen. Pierce skewers into base between trees. Snip off ends and secure with glue.

6 Using hot glue, attach gold-painted wagon wheel pasta pieces (Before you Begin) end-to-end along upper edge of door topper. Touch up final details on door topper with paint, if necessary. Apply strips of double-sided tape to bottom of door topper and secure in place over door frame. Keep it snug against wall.

# NAPKIN RINGS AND PLACE CARD HOLDERS

*Use polymer clay to make festive table-setting accessories that you can give as take-home gifts.*

## YOU WILL NEED

- ❏ POLYMER CLAY & SEALER
- ❏ ROLLING PIN
- ❏ WAX PAPER
- ❏ CRAFT KNIFE OR CRAFT SCISSORS
- ❏ CARDBOARD & PAPER TOWEL TUBE
- ❏ TOOTHPICKS
- ❏ BAKING SHEET
- ❏ PETROLEUM JELLY
- ❏ WHITE ACRYLIC PAINT (OPTIONAL)

## BEFORE YOU BEGIN

*Create whimsical variations for clay shapes by layering clay into pinwheel, stripe or checker-board designs.*

### Pinwheels

**For pinwheels,** roll out two or more colors of polymer clay into thin sheets, about ⅛ inch to ¼ inch. Layer the sheets while alternating colors. Trim the edges evenly with a craft knife. Roll up the layers to form a log shape. Slice the rolled log crosswise, creating pinwheels.

### Stripes

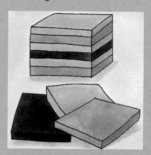

**Roll several colors of** clay into sheets, about ⅛ inch to ¼ inch thick. Stack them while alternating colors until desired number of stripes is achieved. Trim edges and slice stack crosswise. Or wrap outer edge of striped stack with a contrasting color before slicing.

### Checkerboards

**Using two different colors** of ¼-inch-thick clay, cut two 12-inch strips of each color. Lay three strips parallel to each other so that the edges touch (right). Cut strips crosswise into three 4-inch-striped pieces. Stack 4-inch pieces, flipping center layer to alternate color order and create checkerboard; slice.

# MAKING TABLE-SETTING ACCESSORIES

**HANDY HINTS**

If clay seems dry, mix with petroleum jelly for better consistency.

**Add design details** with paints after clay is baked, if desired.

1 Wipe wax paper and tools with petroleum jelly to prevent clay from sticking. Warm clay with hands and knead to pliable consistency. For holly leaves, roll out clay with rolling pin to approximately ⅛-inch thickness.

2 Using prepurchased template or drawing freehand, create cardboard template of leaf shape. Place template on rolled-out clay, then cut around template with craft knife. Remove excess clay from around leaf.

3 Create four or five leaves for each napkin ring desired following directions in Steps 1 and 2. Once leaves have been cut out, draw veins on them with toothpick or craft knife. Carefully set aside to use later.

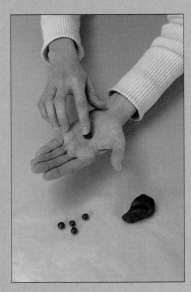

4 Warm and knead red polymer clay. Form small berries by shaping red clay into small balls and rolling between palms. Keep balls of clay moving around hand in a circular motion to keep balls even and smooth.

5 Select four or five leaves. Press end of one leaf to top of next, forming ring around quarter piece of paper towel tube. Add berries to stem of last leaf placed on tube. Bake on cardboard-covered baking sheet at no higher than 225 degrees for 15 to 20 minutes; allow to cool. Remove tube by gently slicing through cardboard with craft knife. Add some white acrylic paint to leaves. Coat holly leaves and berries with clay sealer.

6 To make place card holders, position leaves front to back, pinching them together at stems. Add berries to both sides on leaf bottom. Place on cardboard-covered baking sheet and bake at 225 degrees for 15 to 20 minutes.

# FESTIVE STEP STOOL

*Adding a cheerful design to a step stool will enhance any holiday scheme.*

## YOU WILL NEED

- ❑ CHILD'S ADJUSTABLE STEP STOOL/CHAIR
- ❑ ACRYLIC PAINTS
- ❑ FINE-GRADE SANDPAPER
- ❑ 1- & 2-INCH FOAM BRUSHES & FINE-TIP BRUSH
- ❑ TOOTHBRUSH
- ❑ POLYURETHANE
- ❑ PUTTY KNIFE
- ❑ WOOD PUTTY
- ❑ OAKTAG
- ❑ SCISSORS OR CRAFT KNIFE

## BEFORE YOU BEGIN

*Look in unfinished furniture stores or children's shops for child-sized step stools. They are ideal gifts to paint with bright, festive designs for any occasion.*

### Preparing the Surface

Very little preparation is needed when working with an unfinished wooden stool.
• Sand the entire stool surface with a fine-grade sandpaper to remove any rough spots or splinters.
• Use a putty knife to fill any small holes with matching wood putty. Once the putty is dry, sand the surface again.

• If desired, seal the unfinished wood by applying a white water-based primer to the entire stool surface with a 2-inch foam brush.
• Sand again. Remove dust with a lint-free cloth.

### Using the Template

Enlarge the template (right) on a photocopier or graph paper if desired. Using carbon paper and a pencil, transfer the design onto oaktag. Carefully cut out the heart shape with scissors or a craft knife. Then, according to the desired design, trace the oaktag template onto the unpainted seat, back and step with a pencil.

### Finishing Techniques

Speckle the top of the stool with navy paint. In a small dish, thin acrylic paint with water until the paint is a medium consistency.

Dip the bristles of an old toothbrush into the paint. Brush across them with your fingernail, flicking dots of paint onto the stool top.

As a quick finishing technique, sponge the stool top instead. Soften a natural sea sponge by dampening it. Dip the sponge into the water-thinned paint and blot the excess paint onto paper. Sponge across the surface in a random, irregular pattern.

# PAINTING A STEP STOOL

**1** Prepare the surface (Before you Begin). With a 2-inch foam brush, paint each section of the stool, except the back, seat and step, in yellow, red, orange, green or blue. Allow each area to dry completely.

**2** Using the template (Before you Begin) and a pencil, trace hearts. On the back and step, center one on the top slat and two on the bottom. On a 3-slat seat, center one on the top and bottom slats, two on the middle.

**3** Fold the stool into chair position. Using a 1-inch foam brush, apply blue paint around the traced hearts on the stool back and green paint around each heart on the seat; let dry. Paint seat hearts red.

### HANDY HINTS

**For metal stools** or those with metal hinges, use an interior/exterior enamel paint designed specifically for wood and metal surfaces.

### TAKE NOTE

**Test the base paint** for coverage before applying it. If the color is not as intense as you desire, apply a second coat. Or reverse the speckling colors: Use the darker color as the base and the lighter color as the speckle.

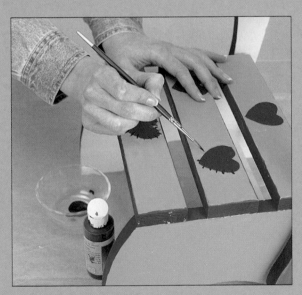

**4** Paint the step section red around the hearts. Paint the hearts on the back and step yellow. Using a fine-tip brush, paint short navy "stitches" around the hearts as if they are sewn on the stool.

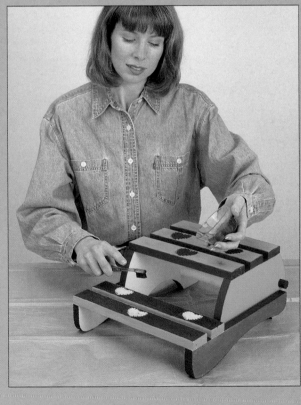

**5** Prepare a small dish of navy paint for speckling (Before you Begin). Using a toothbrush and your finger-nail, apply the paint across the surface of the seat, back, sides and step (the seat back in the folded-down position). Allow all paint to dry completely. To protect the painted design, apply clear polyurethane over all of the painted surfaces.

# PRETTY PAINTED BASKETS

*Give gifts in these pretty baskets. The baskets themselves become part of the gift!*

## BEFORE YOU BEGIN

*A painted wooden basket combines functionality with decorative effect. Choose a color or design that suits the holiday or time of year.*

### From Functional to Focal Point

**Give a basket** a festive winter feeling with a blue background and a random display of snowflakes. Use colored stains instead of paint for a more rustic look. Use this basket for storing hats, gloves and scarves.

**A combination** of roses, tulips and daisies gives a plain basket a romantic, country feel. Create a beautiful display by filling it with a variety of fresh, dried or silk flowers, or small potted plants in terra-cotta pots.

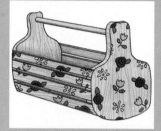

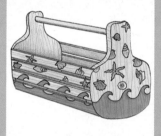

**What better way** to display your treasures from the ocean than in a basket painted with a seaside motif? Keep the basket a natural color and paint waves along the bottom. Add seashells and animals along the sides.

### Stencil Making

Enlarge this star template (below) to two desired sizes. Trace the star onto acetate or stencil film and cut around the outline with a sharp craft knife.

# PAINTING THE BASKET

### HANDY HINTS

**Paints are sold** in a variety of forms. Paint pens offer great control when painting small, detailed designs. Latex paints are very easy to work with, while acrylics offer more vivid colors.

1 Use the foam brush to paint the inside and outside of the basket with the chosen colors; paint the slats first and then the ends. Alternate the color of the slats: red and then white, for example. Don't overfill the brush or let the paint drip between the slats.

2 Use a foam brush to paint the basket ends a cheerful shade of blue; let dry. Use spray adhesive to center the large star template on one end of the box. Fill in with white paint; let dry before removing the stencil; repeat at the other end.

3 Use the smaller star template to stencil white stars around the large stars. Paint more small stars on the slats of the basket, using white paint on the red slats and blue paint on the white slats. Allow the paint to dry completely.

4 Sand the basket lightly and apply one or two coats of clear polyurethane. Polyurethane is not necessary, but it does help protect the painted pattern from dirt and moisture and adds a light sheen to the basket.

# CRACKLE-PAINTED SNOWMAN GOURDS

*Decorative crackle-painted characters make great holiday gifts.*

## BEFORE YOU BEGIN

*To save time and keep the process simple, purchase plastic gourds or papier-mâché eggs found at a crafts store.*

### How to Crackle-Paint

**First, prime all pieces.** Paint each primed piece with a base coat of acrylic paint. This base coat is the color that will show through the crackled top coat.

**Then, apply the clear** crackle medium. The medium will interact with the top coat and cause it to crack and shrink, exposing the base coat color.

**Finally, apply** the top coat color and watch it crackle. Follow the manufacturer's instructions for the appropriate drying times between layers of paint.

### Dressing the Snowmen

The snowmen's outfits can be made easily from fabric scraps, bits of felt or ribbon, or even old clothing.
- Small buttons or peppercorns are perfect for gluing down the front of each snowman (below left).
- For another hat idea, find small feathers and glue them to a felt circle.
- Create a shovel from two layers of aluminum foil folded over a 1-inch square of cardboard and a toothpick handle glued to one side.

- For earmuffs, glue two pom-poms to a piece of pipe cleaner (below right).
- Cut strips of fabric 12 by 1½ inches to make a scarf.
- Make ice skates to sling over a twig arm from cardboard, glue and string.
- Fashion a corncob pipe from black construction paper and glue it to the side of the snowman's mouth.
- Dollhouse accessories make perfect finishing touches.

# MAKING CRACKLE-PAINTED SNOWMEN

**HANDY HINTS**

Real, hollow gourds may be used instead of plastic. The gourds should be dried and sealed with polyurethane before applying the crackle medium.

Either drill with a small bit or carefully screw in small screws to make holes for the twig arms. Glue in place to secure.

1 Select plastic gourds or papier-mâché eggs of various sizes. Following manufacturer's instructions, paint the gourds with a primer or flat white paint. Let the gourds dry completely before applying a base coat.

2 Paint the shapes with a tan base coat. Allow to dry. Paint each gourd with a clear crackle medium; let dry. Paint on a white top coat, and as it dries, it will begin to crackle. Be careful not to smear coats while drying.

3 Cut the twigs with a craft knife into small pieces for the arms. After each gourd has dried completely, make a hole on each side for the arm placement. Glue the twigs in place using a glue gun.

4 Paint small dots for the eyes and mouth and glue the buttons on the front of each snowman. Cut off the end of a toothpick for a "carrot" nose. Paint the toothpick tip orange before gluing it onto the face.

5 On the snowman, add a scarf, earmuffs and a corncob pipe to finish (Before you Begin). For the smaller snowman, add earmuffs, a scarf and a shovel. Glue cotton balls around the base of each snowman for added stability when standing. If desired, make a third snowman with feminine accessories for a complete trio.

# Napkins for Special Celebrations

*Give these custom-painted napkins and let the celebrations begin.*

## BEFORE YOU BEGIN

*When choosing a fabric color for napkins, keep in mind that stains are more noticeable on white and pastel napkins, while darker napkins tend to disguise stains more easily. Wash all painted napkins with a gentle detergent.*

### Cutting the Napkins

Use purchased linen or cotton napkins or make your own napkins from a firmly woven fabric. Paint a custom design to coordinate with a special decorating theme.

Most standard cocktail napkins are 6 to 8 inches square. Dinner napkins can be 16 to 20 inches square. Whatever size napkins you decide to make, add 1 inch to the finished length and width measurements for hem allowances.

### Stitching the Napkins

To form the hem, fold all sides of the square under ½ inch and press flat. With a sewing machine and matching thread, stitch around the sides, ¼ inch from folded edge. Trim hem close to stitching line (below).

To finish, fold all sides under ½ inch again and press flat. From the wrong side, topstitch along the inner fold around all sides of the napkin (below).

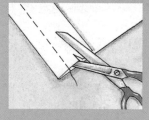
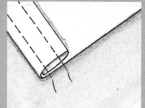

### Painting Tips

• Prewash napkins, both handmade and purchased, before painting to remove sizing. This lets paint seep into the weave instead of lying on top of fabric.
• Always test paint on a scrap of fabric. Avoid shaking the bottle. Drag the tip across the fabric for a smooth finish.
• If desired, mix fabric paints to create custom colors. Do not add water to the mixture or the paint will bleed on the fabric.

# PAINTING A NAPKIN

**OOPS**

**When painting,** do not wipe drips and spills from the napkin. This will only smear the paint. Instead, lift the paint from the fabric with the tip of a paper towel until most of the paint is gone. Wet a cotton swab with a mild detergent-and-water solution and dab it over the spot. Change swabs and continue dabbing until the paint is gone.

1 Cover a flat surface with a piece of protective paper, then lay hemmed napkin on top, right side up. With a pencil, lightly mark confetti placement by randomly drawing small dots all over the napkin.

2 With a small paintbrush, paint gold and silver confetti by dabbing brush over marks. Slightly drag the brush against the napkin for square confetti shapes; pounce the brush tip lightly to make circles.

3 With a steady hand, paint gold streamers randomly on the napkin. Lightly squeeze the paint bottle to create a steady, even flow and carefully move your hand in a circular direction while making the squiggles.

4 When dry, paint the edges of the napkin, from the stitching line to the folded edge, with gold fabric paint. Be careful not to smear the paint on one side while painting the edge on another; let dry.

5 Lay the napkin facedown on a protected flat surface and cover it with a press cloth. With iron on a warm setting, press the napkin to heat-set the painted design. Repeat steps for remaining napkins.

# SCENTED SEASONAL DISPLAY

*Evoke the spirit of the season with the gift of a fragrant table arrangement.*

## YOU WILL NEED

- ❑ 2½-INCH-DIAMETER BIRCH BRANCH
- ❑ ESSENTIAL OILS
- ❑ UNSCENTED OIL
- ❑ BAY LEAVES & RAFFIA
- ❑ DRIED ORANGE SLICES, NUTS & BERRIES
- ❑ DRILL & ¼-INCH DRILL BIT
- ❑ HANDSAW & NEEDLE
- ❑ SPRAY BOTTLE & BOWL
- ❑ CANDLES & PLATE
- ❑ PINECONES
- ❑ MOSS

## BEFORE YOU BEGIN

*Create your own custom fragrances by mixing naturally scented dried materials with scented oils.*

### The Essentials of Oils

Essential oils are highly concentrated oils derived from specific plants such as bayberry and grapefruit.
• Essential oils can be purchased from health food and craft stores.
• For strong scents, mix pure oils and mist over dried natural materials.

• For light scents, mist a few drops of scented oil with ¼ cup of grapeseed oil or another unscented oil.
• For best results, let the scented materials cure in an airtight container for at least one week; if time permits, let the mixture cure for six weeks.

### Planning the Garland

**Freshly cut birch** has a clean, aromatic scent. Scout out small (2½ inches in diameter), fallen birch branches on a walk in the woods or look for them in your backyard; one long branch should be plenty. Using a handsaw, cut the 2½-inch birch branch into ⅜-inch-thick discs (right). If desired, cut the discs at an angle to create interesting elliptical shapes and

varied textures. You can also buy precut discs from a craft store and some lumberyards.

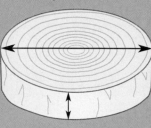

**If desired, use nuts and dried berries** to add festive color and texture to the

winter garland. For the best results, attach the nuts and dried berries to a disc that has a predrilled hole in the center (left). Hot-glue the dried berries and nuts to both flat sides of the disc to cover.

# MAKING A SCENTED BIRCH GARLAND

1 Position a birch disc on top of a hard work surface. Hold the edge of the disc with one hand, and with a ¼-inch drill bit, drill a hole through the center. Continue to drill center holes through remaining birch discs.

2 Mix essential oils with unscented oil to make the desired fragrance. Pour the oils into a spray bottle and mist the dried natural materials. Stir the materials to ensure that all pieces are misted.

3 Poke holes through dried materials with a needle. Thread the dried materials onto two strands of 36-inch-long raffia. Alternate between birch discs, orange slices, bay leaves and discs with nuts and berries.

4 Continue to make a 12-inch-diameter garland. When complete, tie the ends of the raffia together to secure. Tie the remaining raffia pieces together into a bow, then fasten the bow to one side of the garland.

5 Position the garland around a plate. Place an assortment of candles in the center to complete the display—the heat from the candles will activate the scent. Finish by placing pinecones and moss around the candles to disguise the plate.

# PAINTED MIRROR FRAME

*Give a gaily painted mirror frame to help someone celebrate the changing seasons.*

## BEFORE YOU BEGIN

*Whether painting a new frame or recycling an old one, be sure the frame is wide enough for your design.*

### Preparing the Frame

Look for a frame that has a border of equal width. Divide the frame borders into four squares of equal measurement. If the frame is not of equal width, adjust the design accordingly.
• If needed, sand the joints of unfinished wooden frames to even the surface. Wipe with a damp cloth before applying primer.
• Always prime prepainted surfaces. If the surface is peeling, cracked or irregular, strip the old paint, sand the surface and then carefully wipe with a damp cloth.

### The Design Template

**Adjust the tree** and snowflake designs (right) to fit your frame. Measure the width of the frame to determine the pattern size desired. For a balanced look, the width of the tree should equal approximately half of the frame width.

**Enlarge the design** on a photocopier to the desired size. To transfer the design to oaktag, place a piece of graphite paper between the design and oaktag and trace with a pencil. Cut the tree out to make a template.

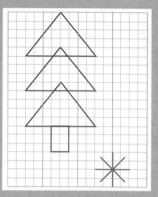

**When tracing** the tree onto the frame, create a design where only parts of the tree are showing. This keeps the design from being too rigid.

### Installing the Mirror

**Attach two sawtooth** hangers to the upper corners of the back of the mirror frame. Insert two screws on the back of both the upper and lower frame edges to hold the mirror in place.

**Apply duct** or electrical tape along all four edges of the mirror to secure it.

# PAINTING THE FRAME

**HANDY HINTS**

Spray the matte finish varnish evenly to avoid drips or uneven coats. If needed, sand lightly and apply another layer.

A hardware store that sells glass can also cut a mirror to size for you if needed.

1 With a wide, flat paintbrush, apply a white base coat over the entire surface of the frame, including the side and inner edges. For an even surface, apply a second base coat on the front of the frame; let dry.

2 With pencil and ruler, mark the corner square lines, extending from the inner to outer frame edges; mark center squares. Apply masking tape along the outside edges of the pencil lines and paint blue; let dry.

3 Trace the template (Before you Begin) on the frame. Create a random yet balanced pattern, with an entire tree appearing on both sides. With a small paintbrush, paint the trees dark blue; let dry.

4 Using the small paintbrush, paint white snowflakes on the blue squares and blue snowflakes on the white squares. This creates an even and balanced composition. Allow the frame to dry thoroughly.

5 Seal the design by spraying the entire surface of the frame with a layer of matte finish varnish. Center the mirror facedown over the back opening of the frame and install the mirror (Before you Begin). Hang the frame on the wall.

# Holiday Evergreen Swag

*Create a festive winter decorating gift with a simple outdoor swag.*

## BEFORE YOU BEGIN

*Collect a variety of evergreens to add color and texture to the swag. Condition them before using to ensure that they last a long time.*

### Preparing the Evergreens

- Recut non-woody stems. Submerge stems in warm water/floral preservative solution; leave overnight. Then cut stems to right length at an angle, remove all foliage below waterline and put into clean water until ready to use.
- Recut woody stems, slit them 2 inches with sharp knife, scrape off lower bark and pound stem ends. Repeat procedure above for soaking stems and cutting and cleaning them before use.

### Painting the Birdhouse Ornaments

- Select a variety of brightly colored acrylic paints for decorations.
- Squeeze a small amount of each paint color onto an old plate. This makes painting lots of little pieces go much faster.
- Use a small paintbrush to apply paint to the bird-houses. Keep the decorations simple, or add more elaborate details such as windows and doors, if desired.
- When paint is dry, seal with polyurethane.

# CRAFTING AN EVERGREEN SWAG

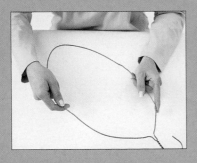

**1** Leaving hook in place, bend body of a sturdy metal hanger into an oval shape. Seal hanger with a coat of polyurethane or wrap with florist's tape to prevent rusting when it hangs outdoors.

**2** Mold piece of chicken wire or florist's mesh over molded hanger shape. Using florist's wire, fasten down edges so they are secure. Make sure no pointed edges of wire protrude.

**3** Combine various greens to make bunches. Use about five sprigs for each bunch. Wrap florist's wire about 2 to 3 inches from base of stems. Twist ends of wire to hold bunches securely.

### HANDY HINTS

**Hot-glue a soft** fabric backing to the swag to prevent the florist's wire from causing damage to the surface below.

### TAKE NOTE

**When wiring the** stems together to make a bundle, make them more secure by twisting the bundle rather than twisting the florist's wire.

**4** Beginning at bottom of wire frame, wire bunches securely onto frame. Start in middle and work outward; work toward top of frame, positioning all bunches with stems up.

**5** At top of swag frame, reverse position of bunches, wiring them on upside down. Position bunches so their unsecured ends are fanning outward to spread around top of swag. Make sure greens conceal top of hanger hook. Fill in swag frame completely so none of mesh is visible.

**6** Wire birdhouses in place with florist's wire. Make sure they are wired onto a secure bunch, or pull wire all the way through to frame underneath.

**7** Tie a bow in middle of ribbon. Wrap ribbon into swag, covering area where stem placement changes direction. Weave ribbon in and out of birdhouses and bundles of greenery. If ribbon will not stay in place, use hot glue to secure. Use coat hanger hook to hang swag in place.

# Quilted Holiday Wall Hanging

*Machine stitching simplifies old-fashioned patchwork for this handcrafted gift.*

## You Will Need

- ❏ Scraps of coordinating cotton prints
- ❏ Rotary cutter & cutting mat
- ❏ 2 yards white fabric
- ❏ ¼ yard matching fabric for borders
- ❏ Quilt batting
- ❏ Sewing machine
- ❏ Matching thread
- ❏ Scissors & pins
- ❏ Bias tape
- ❏ Wooden dowel

## BEFORE YOU BEGIN

*Once you learn the basic steps, patchwork is one of the easiest quilting techniques to master.*

### Basics of Quick Piecing

Machine stitching speeds the process of patchwork.
- Cut pieces the exact size. A rotary cutter will simplify cutting.
- Keep seams aligned so the pieced design will be accurate when complete.

- Use a ¼-inch seam.
- Stitch pieces together in sequential order, preferably in rows.
- Machine quilt the design by stitching through all layers, following the lines of the patchwork design.

### Cutting Pattern Pieces

**Pieced hearts:** Cut 19 2½-inch squares from various coordinating cotton prints. Cut two of the squares into four triangles.

**Background for heart:** Cut one 5-inch square for the corner and four 2½- by 10½-inch border strips. Cut two 2½-inch squares from white background fabric; cut into four triangles.

**Sashing:** Cut four 2½- by 14½-inch pieces (A) and one 2½- by 46½-inch strip (B).

**Border strips:** Cut two 2½- by 30½-inch strips (C) and two 2½- by 50½-inch strips (D).

**Backing:** Cut muslin fabric to 39½ by 46½ inches.

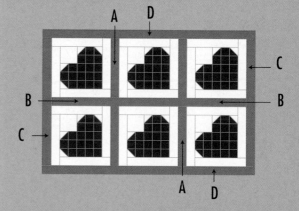

### Making Bias Tape

**From background** fabric, cut 4½-inch bias strips, piecing to equal 6 yards; cut into two 50-inch and two 72-inch strips.

**With wrong sides** facing, fold bias tape in half lengthwise—along long sides; press flat.

# SEWING A QUILTED WALL HANGING

**1** With right sides facing and raw edges aligned, form square by stitching background triangle to heart triangle (Before you Begin). Repeat to make four squares.

**2** Using template (Before you Begin), stitch squares together in rows. Iron seams flat, alternating direction by rows. Stitch top two rows together; add large square.

**3** With right sides facing and raw edges aligned, stitch rows together to make heart. Be sure raw edges match. Press flat, following seam direction.

## HANDY HINTS

**Sign and date** your pieced wall hanging by writing on the back with a permanent fabric pen. Press with a hot iron to seal the ink.

**Always pin seams** together before stitching to ensure accurate alignment and to avoid creating uneven squares.

## DOLLAR SENSE

**Recycle fabric scraps** by using them to make patchwork squares. For best results, combine fabrics from the same color family.

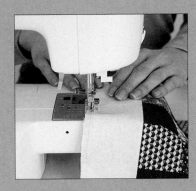

**4** Stitch border strips (Before you Begin) to sides, then to top and bottom of pieced square. Repeat process to make total of six pieced hearts.

**5** Lay hearts on flat surface in two rows of three, with bottoms pointing right. Pin sashing pieces (Before you Begin), right sides facing, to hearts' inner sides.

**6** Stitch sashing in place along sides. With right sides facing, stitch long border pieces to top, middle and bottom edges, then to sides of heart sections.

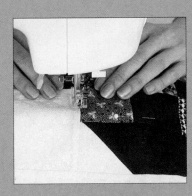

**7** Stack backing, batting and pieced front together; pin in place. Topstitch ¼ inch from border edges, then along seams of pieced heart and sashing.

**8** With right sides facing and raw edges aligned, stitch bias tape around sides, then around top and bottom of wall hanging. Miter corners.

**9** Fold bias to back, turn edges under and slipstitch. Cut 4- by 42-inch casing; turn edges under and slipstitch in place. Insert wooden dowel in casing to hang on wall.

# GIFTS FOR
# DISPLAY &
# STORAGE

*The best gifts are often the ones the recipients can show off proudly … and remember fondly every time they look at them. That's what you'll find in this chapter—gift items made to be displayed and shared around the home. Many of these ideas center around picture frames and other ways to display photos; let the gift-getter insert an image … or include one in that's meaningful to both of you! You'll also find many other ideas here, from birdhouses and hat boxes to painted jars, decorative pots, mailboxes for creative storage, and much more. Display your talents!*

# SPATTER-PAINTED PICTURE FRAMES

*Spatter painting creates subtle, distinct finishes on frames you want to give as gifts.*

## BEFORE YOU BEGIN

*The factors that determine the spattering effects are how much paint is on the brush, the distance the brush is held from the surface and how fast you move your hand over the surface.*

### The Effects of Spatter Painting

**A loaded paintbrush** will create large dots. For finer dots, use less paint or spatter on paper first.

**The closer your** hand is to the surface, the finer the dots will be. The dots become larger as you move farther away from the surface.

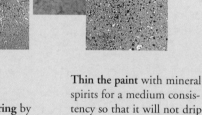

**In addition,** the consistency of the paint and the number of different paint colors used will also affect the look of the finished project.

**Avoid overspattering** by moving your hand across the surface while flicking the brush.

**Practice these techniques** on paper to learn how to change both the pressure of your fingertip and angle of the tool.

**Thin the paint** with mineral spirits for a medium consistency so that it will not drip or lump.

**Add new twists** to basic spattering by masking designs like vertical lines (above center) or panels, or by spattering more than one paint color over a base coat (above left).

### Prep Work

Spattering, also known as splattering and flyspecking, can be achieved by using various types of tools found around the house.
• Hit the handle of a brush against a flat stick or palette knife.

• For a fine finish, drag your thumb along an old toothbrush or run the toothbrush over a fine metal screen.
• Move a loaded stencil brush along the teeth of a comb.

# SPATTER PAINTING A FRAME

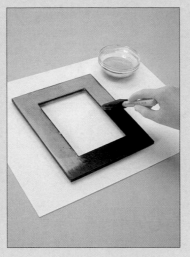

## HANDY HINTS

To **disguise** an uneven finish, apply a matte polyurethane over a surface painted with flat paint. Use a glossy polyurethane for a polished finish.

## TAKE NOTE

**Do not mix** oil and acrylic paints. This causes the paint to puddle and keeps it from spreading evenly over the surface.

**Avoid overloading** the brush with paint. Otherwise, when you flick paint from the brush, the paint dots will run together.

1 Paint frame with base coat of paint; let dry. Lightly sand frame with steel wool until smooth. Rub linseed oil over frame to give it a slight sheen and to keep glaze from spreading uncontrollably.

2 To make glaze, mix one part oil paint with two parts mineral spirits to achieve a consistency similar to milk. With a sponge brush, apply light layer of glaze over front of frame. Do not glaze frame's inside or sides.

3 Dip stiff stencil brush into straight mineral spirits, then brush fingertip against brush tip to flick mineral spirits onto frame. Begin at one corner, moving brush slowly around frame to create even spatters.

4 When frame is completely covered with spatters, use a clean cloth to gently press mineral spirits down into glaze. Apply another coat of base color, or use a contrasting color, to sides and inside of frame. When dry, coat frame with matte polyurethane; let dry.

# COLLECTIBLE BIRDHOUSES

*Create endless varieties of birdhouses from one simple pattern, and give a unique birdhouse to each recipient.*

## BEFORE YOU BEGIN

*Assembling a birdhouse couldn't be easier. The only hard part is deciding how to decorate it. Try the log cabin look described below, or paint any type of design onto the wooden house.*

### Preparing Birdhouse Pieces

- Purchase a 4- or 8-foot lengh of 1x10 clear pine or poplar.
- After the milling process, a 1x10 board will actually measure ¾ by 8½ inches. The pattern (below) reflects this dimensional change.
- Some lumberyards will cut pieces to the right size.
- Use hot glue for indoor birdhouses. Use wood glue with 1½-inch finishing nails for outdoor use and polyurethane for a protective seal.
- Use a right-angled ruler; measure and mark two roofs, two ends, two sides and one base piece onto the surface of the 1x10. Follow the pattern shown below.
- Using a power saw, cut all pieces. You can use a handsaw, but the process is time-consuming.
- Label each piece.
- Drill a hole in one end piece, even with the roofline, using an electric drill fitted with a 1¼-inch bit. If you do not have a drill, check with a full-service lumberyard—they may be able to do it for you.

| 8½" | 8½" | 5¼" | 5¼" | 5¼" | 5¼" | 5½" |
|-----|-----|-----|-----|-----|-----|-----|
| ROOF | ROOF | END | END | SIDE | SIDE | BASE |

### Assembly Tips

The birdhouse sides and ends are assembled around a base to form the body of the house. One narrow and one wide roof piece are glued at right angles to create equal lengths of peak when assembled.

# BUILDING A BIRDHOUSE

**1** Apply glue to sides at short ends. Attach to front end board with edges flush. Apply glue to remaining side ends and all ends of base; assemble body of house. Apply glue to long end of smaller roof piece. Attach to longer roof piece, edges flush.

**2** Paint outside of house and roof separately, first with one coat of primer then one or more coats of paint. Sand lightly between coats. Optional: Using a pencil, draw outline of one or several rectangular windows on sides of house.

**3** Cut twigs to fit sides and ends of house. Cut twigs to follow peak of roof and around hole and window. Apply glue to twigs; position horizontally to cover house, spacing as close as possible. Fill in open spaces with very thin twigs.

## HANDY HINTS

If you want to design a large or intricate birdhouse, consider testing the design by making a prototype from foam core before using wood.

## DOLLAR SENSE

Save a few dollars and select a lesser quality wood for those houses that will be completely covered by twigs or flowers.

**4** Using a craft knife, cut scales from pinecones. Starting at lower roof edge and working in vertical rows, glue scales to roof. Apply glue to roof; press pinecone piece to wood. Overlap scale ends to resemble roofing shingles.

**5** Apply glue to peak of house and attach roof. Or eliminate glue for easy lid removal if house will be used as a storage container. Optional: Using a light color, paint window frame on house sides. Decorate corners by adding silk or dried flowers.

# FABRIC-COVERED HAT BOXES

*Cover a plain hat box with fabric to create a stylish storage accessory—a gift anyone would love.*

## BEFORE YOU BEGIN

*Select a box and lid that are sturdy enough to hold their shape during fabric application. Gift shops and craft shops sell suitable boxes, or you can make your own from smooth, heavy cardboard.*

### Measuring the Box

To ensure the hat box and lid are completely covered with fabric, make sure you have obtained all these measurements before you begin:

• Use a tape measure to measure the height of the main body of the box. Measure the circumference of the main body of the box (below).

• Measure the height and circumference of the box lid (right).

• Add 2 inches to each measurement.

• Using adjusted measurements, mark two rectangles on paper side of fusible web. Cut out rectangles.

• Example: If the box is 6 inches high with a 44-inch circumference and a 1½-inch-high lid, the rectangles will measure 46 by 8 inches and 46 by 3½ inches.

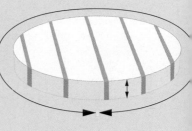

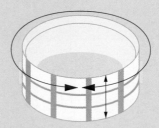

### Preparing the Box

**Wipe the box clean** of any dust or dirt. Make sure that all edges are smooth.

**If the box** is dark or has dark printing on it, paint it with white latex to prevent show-through.

**The lid should fit** closely, but not tightly, since the fabric will add thickness to the box and lid.

**Fabric spray adhesive** can be used in place of fusible web. However, spray adhesive dries very quickly, making it difficult to rectify mistakes. Fabric glue is another suitable substitute.

# COVERING A HAT BOX WITH FABRIC

1 Remove backing from fusible web rectangles. Position rectangles on wrong side of fabric with other paper side facing out. Fuse rectangles in place with iron according to manufacturer's instructions.

2 Cut out larger rectangle; remove paper backing. Wrap rectangle around box with 1 inch extending at top and bottom edges. Fix fabric to box by fusing it with tip of iron as you wrap. Ends will overlap.

3 Finger-press extending fabric at top edge to inside of box. Use tip of iron to fuse fabric in place. Work around circumference of box, holding box on its side and easing excess fabric to lie smoothly.

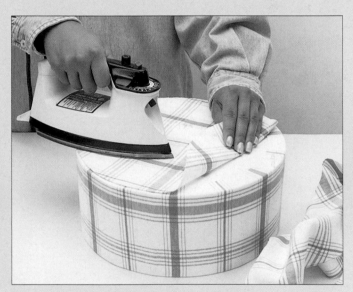

4 Finish bottom of box by clipping extended fabric at 1-inch intervals from raw edge to box edge. Finger-press and smooth clipped edges to bottom of box. Fuse in place with tip of iron. Repeat Steps 1 through 4 for box lid.

5 Using a pencil, lightly trace bottom of box and top of lid onto paper side of fusible web; cut out fusible web circles; repeat with fabric. Fuse circular web pieces to wrong side of fabric with paper side facing out.

6 Cut out fabric circles; remove paper backing from fusible web. Position fabric circle on bottom of box, centering it so that it covers all clipped edges. Fuse circle in place. Fuse second circle in place on top of box lid. If fabric is not adhering to box properly, apply a few dabs of hot glue where needed. Hot glue can also be used to help prevent fabric from fraying around edges.

# CUSTOMIZED PHOTO MATS

*Create a picture gallery custom-made for special photos. Commemorate a special trip or event ... or an entire friendship!*

## YOU WILL NEED

- ❏ FRAME & PHOTOS
- ❏ POSTER BOARD (BLUE & WHITE)
- ❏ LIGHTWEIGHT PAPER (GOLD)
- ❏ TRACING PAPER
- ❏ WHITE CARDBOARD
- ❏ ARTIST'S KNIFE
- ❏ FELT-TIPPED PEN
- ❏ RULER & GLUE
- ❏ PENCIL & ERASER

## BEFORE YOU BEGIN

*Choose a ready-made frame and colored poster board to set off photographs. A double layer of poster board gives this project a professional finish.*

### Frames and Poster Board

Use ready-made frames and arrange your photographs to suit the shape.

• Thick mat board is difficult to cut, so use poster board.

• Two layers of poster board, with the windows outlined in felt-tipped pen, give an illusion of depth—like the mitered edges of professional mats.

### Cutting Techniques

**Cut around the glass** or acrylic plastic supplied with the frame to get the outer dimensions for the mat. Measure how much the frame overlaps the front of the glass and take this into account when planning the photo layout.

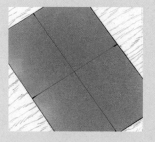

**To center the photos,** find the middle of the mat. Measure and mark the center points of each outside edge, then join the opposite points to make a cross. For a symmetrical design, measure out from this center point to mark the windows.

**Practice cutting circular** windows on scrap paper. Mark the circle using a compass or by drawing around a glass or dish. Using an artist's knife, cut a cross shape in the center, then make four curved cuts to remove the window.

# CUTTING THE PAPER MAT

**1** Start by selecting your favorite family photographs. Lay tracing paper over the pictures and draw squares and circles on the tracing paper to see which window shape will best suit the photos.

**2** After deciding on the best size for each window, cut shapes from white cardboard to use as templates. Arrange them on the poster board. Use leftover cardboard strips to indicate where frame will be.

**3** Make a sketch of the positions of the windows and mark their dimensions. Use the sketch to mark the windows on the lightweight gold paper. Cut out the windows on the gold sheet using an artist's knife.

**HANDY HINTS**

**Use an artist's knife** with a fine point for the best results. Always cut away from the hand that you are using to hold the paper steady.

**QUICK FIX**

**If the windows** are a little rough around the edges after cutting them, smooth the paper down carefully with an emery board.

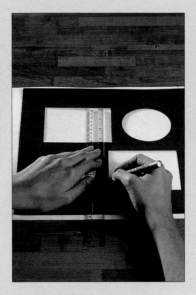

**4** Place the gold paper right side up over the blue poster board, also right side up. Trace through the gold windows so they reappear on the blue. Mark and cut the blue windows so they are ⅛ inch larger all around.

**5** Draw outlines around the windows with a felt-tipped pen. Mark straight lines with a ruler. For curves, use a glass, dish or compass. Paste the two mats together at each corner, blue on top of gold.

**6** Place the finished mat over the white backing paper that is supplied with the frame. Hold it firmly in place and then trace around the inside edges of each of the windows with pencil. Apply a thin layer of glue to the backs of the photos and press them on the shapes that are drawn. Position the mat on top of the backing paper and then frame.

# MOUNTED COLLECTIBLE DISPLAYS

*Turn dimensional treasures or knickknacks into a special gift your friends will love to display.*

## YOU WILL NEED

❏ BUTTONS OR OTHER
  COLLECTIBLES
❏ SHADOW BOX FRAME
❏ MAT BOARD
❏ GRAPH PAPER
❏ PENCIL & METAL
  RULER
❏ CRAFT KNIFE
❏ ⅛-INCH GRAPHIC ART
  TAPE
❏ HOT GLUE GUN
❏ FOAM BOARD
❏ DOUBLE-SIDED TAPE

## BEFORE YOU BEGIN

*To create a long-lasting display that doesn't damage the collection, adapt a mounting method to suit the collectible being displayed.*

### Preparing the Mounting Board

**Before purchasing** a shadow box, measure the depth of your thickest collectible to ensure the box is deep enough to fit.

**Arrange the items** on a table in the form in which they will be displayed; measure the collection to see what size frame you need.

**For frame sizes** and collectibles that seem mismatched, consider grouping the collectibles toward the center of the mat and allowing a wide border on all edges.

**For bottle caps,** tiny toys and other oddly shaped collectibles, use a tacky clay intended to hold dollhouse miniatures in place.

**For sew-through buttons** or fabric collectibles that may be destroyed by glue, use a small nail to hammer two holes ¼ inch apart at each X marking. Sew the button or fabric to the mounting board.

**For butterflies,** labels and other delicate collectibles, use mounting pins to hold them in place.

**For shank buttons,** use a large nail to hammer one hole at each X marking (below left). Apply glue to the button shank and insert it into the hole (below right).

### Other Choices

Just about any favorite item can be made into an interesting framed display.
• Champagne and wine cork collections are becoming popular for those who want to preserve memories of a favorite place or occasion.

• A collection of leaves or bugs is an inexpensive and informative science project for a child's first collection.
• Sparkling earrings and beads make a truly glamorous display inside a shiny silver frame.

# MOUNTING COLLECTIBLES

1 Lay out buttons on graph paper to determine dimensions of grid. Draw grid on graph paper. Draw crosses inside each square on grid to find exact centers.

2 Following graph paper dimensions, mark grid on mat board cut to fit frame. Define lines with black graphic art tape. Cut tape ends even with a craft knife.

3 For best effect, arrange buttons on grid so shapes, colors and sizes complement each other. Apply small dab of hot glue to button backs and mount in center of boxes at markings. Hold each button in place for a few seconds to allow glue to dry. Refer to Before you Begin for mounting buttons with a shank or other types of collectibles.

4 Place finished button arrangement in frame. For frames without a recessed mounting slot, position a spacer between glass and board to hold buttons away from glass. Cut a strip of foam board and attach to frame using double-sided tape.

# PAINTED GLASS STORAGE JARS

*Storage jars make perfect canvases for simple, hand-painted designs ... and the end results make perfect gifts. Fill them with something special!*

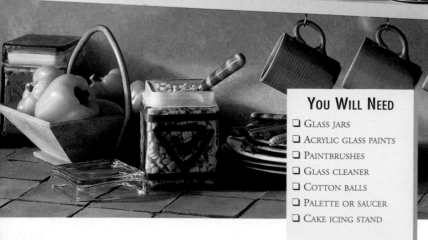

## YOU WILL NEED

- ❏ GLASS JARS
- ❏ ACRYLIC GLASS PAINTS
- ❏ PAINTBRUSHES
- ❏ GLASS CLEANER
- ❏ COTTON BALLS
- ❏ PALETTE OR SAUCER
- ❏ CAKE ICING STAND

## BEFORE YOU BEGIN

*Start with glass paints in a variety of colors, and brushes in different sizes. Then try out the designs on recycled, clean jelly jars before painting on the actual storage jars.*

### Choosing and Using Paints

- Paints designed for use on glass are usually acrylic (water-based). They may be translucent or opaque.
- The finished jars should be baked in the oven according to the paint manufacturer's instructions for a long-lasting finish.
- Not all brands of paint are completely dishwasher-safe, so this project is not suitable for glass jars that are washed regularly. However, storage jars do not need to be put in the dishwasher very often.
- Because the paint is applied to the outside of the jars, there is no need to worry that it will come into contact with food.

### Painting Tips

**Experiment with paint** before starting work, using a selection of good quality brushes in different sizes. Make dots of color with round brushes; paint bands with flat brushes. Use a small, round brush to paint zigzags. Get the feel of the brushes by painting the shapes on scrap paper first.

**Bands of color** can be drawn freehand while turning the jars on a cake icing stand. For straighter, more even lines, mask off portions of the glass jars with tape. Paint between the taped lines. Then wait until paint dries before removing tape so it doesn't get smudged.

# PAINTING THE JARS

**1** Use cotton balls and glass cleaner to clean the outside of the jars. They must be completely dry and free of grease before painting. Avoid handling the jars too much after they have been cleaned.

**2** Choose the color and pattern to paint. Mix the colors on a palette or an old saucer. Create varying shades of green by mixing red, green and orange paint together.

**3** Choose a brush width to suit the desired width of the lines. Put plenty of paint on the brush before starting to paint each line. Draw all the green lines first and let them dry before painting the red lines.

### HANDY HINTS

**When choosing jars** to decorate, make sure that any plastic or rubber seals can be removed before painting the jars—the baking process will melt the seals.

### OOPS

**Don't worry** if you make a mistake while painting the storage jars. The paint can be cleaned off with mineral spirits as long as the jars have not been baked.

**5** Continue adding patterns to the jar until the desired effect is achieved. Paint a wide band of color around the neck of the jar to hide the plastic seal. When all the designs have been painted, leave the jar to dry completely. Then apply a second coat of paint over the first designs. Repeat as necessary until all the painted lines are opaque. Bake the jars in the oven according to the directions on the paint label.

**4** To paint bands of color on round jars, place the jar on a cake icing stand—or even a protected record turntable. Then hold the paintbrush steady while rotating the stand to keep the paint lines straight.

# COVERED CLAY POTS

*Decorate plain clay pots with materials from the great outdoors for a rustic and handsome gift.*

## BEFORE YOU BEGIN

*The ways you can decorate clay pots are limitless. Experiment with items ranging from dried leaves and twigs to shells and seed pods.*

### A Peck of Pots

**To prepare terra-cotta** pots, remove any moss or fungus growing on the outside with a scrub brush and disinfectant; rinse clean and let dry.

**Once the surface** of the pot is ready, search for original items that can transform an ordinary pot into something unique.

**Use different types** of rope to create various textures. Spray paint the rope once you have glued it in place around the pot.

**Dried materials** such as small pinecones, sycamore balls and seed pods are all ideal for covering pots. If desired, paint the pot in a neutral color before gluing the decorations in place.

**To layer preserved leaves,** such as eucalyptus, begin by gluing the first row to the bottom of a small clay pot. Continue to add leaves, overlapping them slightly, until the entire pot is covered.

**Hot-glue twigs** around a clay pot, tying a raffia bow around the bottom for an added effect.

**Instead of covering** the entire pot, glue small dried rosebuds around the rim. Leave the base a natural terra-cotta color or paint it to match the rosebuds.

**Cover a pot with glue,** then roll it in fragrant potpourri or loose herbs like lavender and rosemary.

**Once the glue is dry,** preserve covered pots that will be handled frequently by spraying the entire surface with polyurethane.

### Glues to Use

Certain types of glue are best for specific projects.
- Clear-drying, white craft glue works best for attaching loose herbs and dried flowers to a pot. It is also ideal for keeping eucalyptus leaves in place.

- Heavy items, such as rope, pinecones and large shells should be hot-glued to a pot.
- Clear silicone is an alternative for securing small nuts and stones to the surface of the pot.

# COVERING A POT

**1** Burn one end of a piece of rope with the flame from a small votive. This will prevent the rope from fraying. Using scissors, trim away part of the burned area, being sure to leave enough to seal the rope.

**2** Beginning at the top rim of the pot and using a glue gun, wrap rope around the terra-cotta pot. Keep the rope coiled tightly around the pot to camouflage the terra-cotta surface underneath.

**3** When the entire pot has been covered with rope, cut the rope and burn the end as done in Step 1. Trim away excess burned area, then tuck the burned end underneath one of the coils; glue in place.

## HANDY HINTS

**When working with** hot glue, apply the glue in small sections and wrap the rope around the pot as you go. This keeps you from burning your fingers on the hot glue.

**Avoid touching the** ends of the rope once you have burned them with a candle.

## DOLLAR SENSE

**Save money by** buying clay pots from a home supply store. Clay pots purchased from a craft or department store can be twice the price.

**If you plan to** cover the entire surface, less expensive plastic pots will also work as the base for covering.

**4** Arrange decorative shells or rope knots on the front of the pot, then hot-glue in place. Overlap shells for a grouping effect. If desired, continue gluing shells to the rope around the rim. Once the glue is dry, pull away the stringy pieces of glue from the pot.

# FABRIC-FRAMED PICTURE

*Fabric livens up an ordinary frame to suit the mood of the photo you want to give.*

## YOU WILL NEED

- ❏ WOOD FRAME
- ❏ MEDIUM-WEIGHT FABRIC
- ❏ FUSIBLE BACKING
- ❏ WHITE GLUE
- ❏ SMALL PAINTBRUSH
- ❏ FABRIC SHEARS
- ❏ THIN SILVER CORDING
- ❏ STRAIGHTEDGE

# BEFORE YOU BEGIN

*Accurate fabric measurements make the task of covering the frame easier, and reduce the chance for an error.*

## Choosing and Measuring Fabric

Choose a durable, medium-weight fabric. Heavy fabrics do not layer well and tend to bunch at the corners.

- Back thinner fabrics with one or two thicknesses of fusible iron-on backing cut narrower than frame.
- Cut down the selected fabric to a piece about twice the size of the frame in width and height for easier handling.
- Clean the frame to remove any traces of dirt or grease so the glue will adhere fabric to the frame.
- If the frame is porous, prime it first so that it will not absorb the glue.

## Cutting the Backing and Fabric

**Place the frame** front side down on a piece of fusible backing. With a pencil, trace the inside and outside edges of frame and then redraw ¼ inch inside both lines (red lines). After cutting, the backing will be narrower than the frame (right).

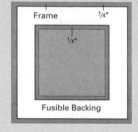

**Lay out fabric** wrong side up on flat surface and center the frame flat side down on top. Trace around the frame with a pencil to outline it on the fabric (red line). Using a straightedge and pencil, measure and mark a distance all around the tracing that is equal to the width of the frame molding plus an additional ¾ inch to allow for the thickness of the frame when wrapping (white line).

Carefully cut out the fabric following the traced lines to make sure the edges of the fabric are even.

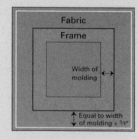

# COVERING A FRAME

**1** Use a small paintbrush to spread a thin, even layer of white glue over the front of the frame.

**2** Place fusible backing on front of frame and smooth down. Let dry. Center frame facedown on wrong side of fabric.

**3** Glue fabric to left outer edge and left back of frame. Hold in place until glue is tacky. Let dry and repeat on right side.

**4** Trim fabric along back surface of frame so only the fabric extending from the front and outer edges remains.

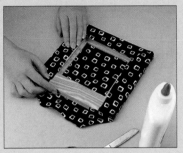

**5** Spread glue on top edge and back of frame. Fold in fabric ends to form triangle and fold to back. Repeat on bottom.

**6** On the fabric covering the opening, draw a square 1 inch in from the edge plus enough to wrap. Trim.

**7** Clip the remaining corners and glue fabric to the inside edge and the back in the same manner.

**8** Cut four lengths of trim. Each length is double the measurement from an inside to an outside corner plus 2 inches.

**9** Glue cording onto frame, placing loop in outside corner. Bring lengths to inside corner and around to the back.

# FABRIC-LINED BASKET

*Easy-to-sew fabric liners brighten household containers, turning them into attractive gifts.*

## BEFORE YOU BEGIN

*A beautiful fabric lining, removable for easy washing, lends style to a laundry basket while preventing garment snags.*

### Measuring and Cutting Fabric

The basket shown here measures 25 inches high and 18 inches in diameter. A liner for a basket this size requires five yards of decorative cording for the drawstring and two yards of fabric (more for matching plaids or pattern repeats).

For the sides, cut two fabric rectangles, each 29½ by 34 inches.

Cut one 19-inch-diameter fabric circle for the bottom of the basket.

If your basket varies in size from the example provided here, modify the fabric dimensions as necessary for a perfect fit.

For the bottom piece, trace around the base of the basket. Add a ½-inch seam allowance all around, and cut out the fabric.

For the main fabric cylinder, cut the fabric wide enough to fit the basket's circumference. Include a 1-inch seam allowance to the height of the basket, plus an additional 9 inches or so to form a collar that folds over the top of the basket.

### Making a Flat-Felled Seam

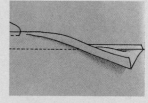

A flat-felled seam gives a neat, professional finish that resists fraying.
• With the wrong sides together, join the fabric with a ½-inch seam.
• Trim one seam allowance to ⅛ inch (above).

• Press the larger seam allowance over the trimmed seam.
• Fold under the raw edge of the full seam allowance, making a neat edge that will cover the trimmed seam (above).
• Stitch the seam allowance in place along the outer folded edge of the fabric.

# SEWING A BASKET LINER

1 Using a flat-felled seam, join the two rectangles of decorative fabric (Before you Begin) for the body of the liner along one long side; press.

2 Join remaining long sides of rectangles with a flat-felled seam, leaving top 9 inches open. Clip to seam line at the 9-inch mark. Apply fray protector to clipped edges.

3 Align open edges above felled side seam and make marks 2¼ and 3¼ inches from the top. Sew ½-inch seam, leaving sides open between marks; press open.

**HANDY HINTS**

For the flat-felled seam that attaches the circular bottom to the fabric cylinder, ease fabric to fit around the circle and sew the seam. Trim the circle's side of the seam, clipping curves. Fold the cylinder portion over the trimmed seam.

4 Press under a ½-inch hem along the upper edge of the fabric cylinder. Pin and stitch the hem in place about ⅜ inch from the top edge of the cylinder; remove pins.

5 Press the top hem under another 1½ inches to form a casing for the drawstring. Pin and stitch in place close to the lower fold. Remove pins and press.

6 For the bottom, pin and sew the 19-inch-diameter fabric piece (Before you Begin) to the fabric cylinder with a flat-felled seam; press. Turn the liner wrong side out.

7 Thread the decorative cording as a drawstring through the casing and knot the ends. Put the liner into the basket, fold the top over the outside and tie the drawstring into a loose, decorative bow.

# DECOUPAGE-ON-GLASS ACCESSORIES

*Inexpensive materials lend elegance to a plain glass bowl and transform it into a beautiful gift.*

## YOU WILL NEED

- ❑ GIFT WRAP
- ❑ SCISSORS
- ❑ MAGAZINES
- ❑ FOAM BRUSH
- ❑ DECOUPAGE GLUE
- ❑ GLASS BOWL
- ❑ DAMP SPONGE

## BEFORE YOU BEGIN

*Vary the look of decoupage on glass by choosing unusual papers and containers. Mason jars, Christmas ornaments and votives all work well.*

### Pick a Paper

Since decoupage is such an easy, inexpensive craft to enjoy, it is fun to experiment with materials you already have at home. Some possibilities include white or yellow telephone directory pages, wallpaper, airmail stationery, newspaper, calendars, catalogs, Sunday comics, illustrations and text from old books, maps, greeting cards and travel brochures.

**For ornaments** or other projects that you want to sparkle, try mixing a little glitter into the glue for the final coat.

### A Touch of Texture

**For smoothest** results when covering curved objects such as bowls, jars or even round ornaments, choose paper that is thin enough to cover the curves without wrinkles or bubbles. Tear the paper into smaller pieces than you would ordinarily use on a flat surface. Use thicker paper on flat items. Patterned or ridged glass will have a pretty texture. Use thin paper so pattern shows through.

# DECOUPAGING A BOWL

**1** Working around the main images, tear fruit-patterned gift wrap into irregularly shaped pieces roughly uniform in size. Tearing the paper gives feathery edges that help one piece blend into the next for a seamless look once the glue is applied.

**2** Cut food-related words (or choose words pertaining to your topic) from magazine pages, making sure the strips are all the same height to form an even border around the rim of the bowl. Cutting shapes yields more definition than tearing.

**3** Using a foam brush, apply a thin coat of decoupage glue to the back of the torn pieces of gift wrap. Stick the glued pieces to the outside of the glass bowl, overlapping the edges slightly. Smooth the pieces with a damp sponge.

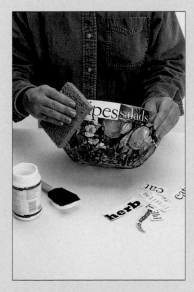

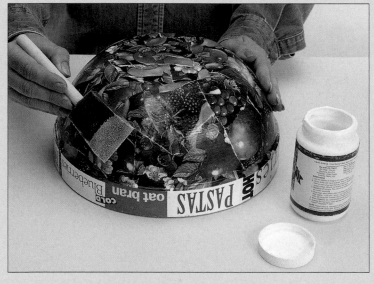

**5** When the paper is completely dry, apply a thin, even coat of decoupage glue to the entire outside of the bowl. Decoupage glue can be thinned with a little water to achieve desired consistency. Decoupage glue, readily available at craft stores, does double duty as an adhesive and a glossy finish coat. Clean up glue spills with a damp cloth as you go; remove dried glue from the work surface with denatured alcohol.

**4** Brush glue onto the back of the magazine word strips and apply them around the rim of the bowl as described in Step 3. Again, smooth the pieces in place and rub out bubbles with a damp sponge. Turn the bowl upside down and leave it to dry.

# HANDCRAFTED RIBBON BOARD

*Turn simple rows of ribbons into a pretty and practical organizer—a gift that anyone will cherish.*

## BEFORE YOU BEGIN

*With this decorative ribbon board, you have the option of tacking items to the board or slipping items between the ribbons, keeping the items free of holes.*

### Preparing the Board

**With a ruler** and utility knife, measure and cut a 20- by 30-inch base from a piece of ½-inch-thick compressed-paper board. On the back, mark two holes on each side of the board for hanger placement; measure 3 inches down from the top, then 3 inches and 4½ inches in. With a ¼-inch drill bit, drill holes completely through the board.

### Selecting Ribbon

**Create visual interest** on your ribbon board by selecting ribbons from the wide variety of textures and colors available (right) to match your decor.

**For instance,** mix florals with both solids and gingham checks for a country look or choose wide satin and velvet bands in subtle tones for a more elegant setting.

**Be sure the ribbon** is durable enough to hold papers, postcards, invitations and other display items. If the ribbon is not stiff enough, or does not have finished edges, an option is to spray it with sizing before beginning the project.

**To determine the** number needed, lay the ribbons across the cut base board. Cut enough ribbons in 24-inch lengths to fill the desired width, allowing for overlaps.

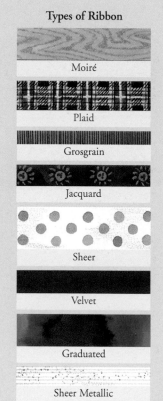

Types of Ribbon

Moiré

Plaid

Grosgrain

Jacquard

Sheer

Velvet

Graduated

Sheer Metallic

# MAKING A RIBBON BOARD

### HANDY HINTS

**Compressed-paper** board, made from recycled newspaper, is available in most hardware stores or lumberyards. It can be substituted with thick foam core or corkboard.

### DOLLAR SENSE

**Because ribbon** can be quite expensive, shop for leftover pieces of ribbon in remnant bins and on bargain tables.

**1** With wire snips, cut two 10-inch-long pieces of 20-gauge wire. For each side, thread one wire piece through holes, from front to back of board (Before you Begin). Twist wire ends together to form a hanger; trim.

**2** Measure and cut a 24- by 34-inch piece of fabric for backing. Lay backing faceup and, using a tape measure, position first ribbon 2 inches from top of backing. Topstitch in place, ⅛ inch from bottom edge only of ribbon.

**3** Pin second ribbon to backing so that top edge overlaps bottom edge of first ribbon; topstitch lower edges in place. Repeat for remaining ribbons. Position last ribbon so it will fold under bottom of board.

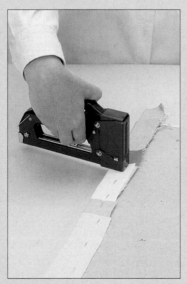

**4** Measure and cut a 33- by 23-inch piece of batting. Lay board in center of batting. Pull batting edges taut to back of board and secure in place with staples. Clip batting at corners to prevent bunching.

**5** Lay fabric facedown, then center board, aligning first ribbon with top of board. Fold fabric over board and staple, working from center out to sides; do not staple corners. Pull fabric taut and staple bottom edge.

**6** Repeat Step 5 for sides of board. Once top, bottom and sides are secure, staple corners. Fold raw edges of corners under, then pull tightly and staple in place. Trim loose threads, if necessary.

# PHOTOS FRAMED WITH GARDEN FLOWERS

*Use dried petals to transform a plain flat frame into a gift that's as pretty as a picture.*

## YOU WILL NEED

❑ DRIED ROSE PETALS
   & DRIED ROSEBUDS
❑ PALE PINK MAT BOARD
❑ GOLD MARKING PEN
❑ GLUE GUN & GLUE
   STICKS
❑ MAT KNIFE & BLADES
❑ RULER & T SQUARE
❑ TWEEZERS
❑ DOUBLE-SIDED TAPE
❑ PENCIL

## BEFORE YOU BEGIN

*To ensure success when creating a floral petal frame, keep the principles of good color mix and good proportion foremost in your mind.*

### Picture Perfect

While it's true that photos of anyone near and dear can pull our heartstrings, a floral-bedecked frame best displays those that are well lit and taken against uncluttered backgrounds. Select only single or double portraits, so your family members and sweethearts will always be shown to their best advantage.

### Rose Selections

**Romantic associations** have long enhanced the beauty of roses. So, use petals from a special occasion to frame a photograph reminiscent of that day.

**Choose rose petal colors** that bring out the colors in the chosen picture.

**Rose petal sizes** vary considerably. Among the smaller are Sweetheart Minuettes. Each rose has 10 to 12 petals, in sizes from ½ inch to 1 inch, making them a fine choice for smaller frames. Larger petaled roses, including those from the centifolia or cabbage rose variety, can have as many as 100 fragrant petals within a single flower head.

### Drying and Sorting Petals

**To preserve roses,** peel off the green sepals at the base of the flower. Remove petals one by one, laying them on a paper towel. Put on gloves, goggles and a mask, then pour a layer of florist's silica crystals on the bottom of an airtight box.

**Using tweezers,** lay rows of petals on the crystals. Gently alternate layers of silica and petals, with a final layer of silica. Close tightly to dry. In three to five days, when petals are no longer pliable, remove them and sort by size on a tray.

# MAKING A ROSE PETAL FRAME

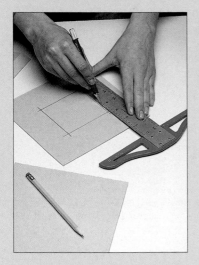

1 Using a T square and pencil, measure a 7- by 7-inch square of mat board; cut with a mat knife. Measure 2 inches in on each side and cut a 5- by 5-inch opening. To form the frame back, cut a second 7-inch square and a 7- by 3-inch triangle prop.

2 Working faceup on the front section, lay the T square just inside one side of the opening and draw a line with a gold marker. Draw lines on the remaining sides to create the grid and corners, as shown.

3 Using the glue gun, apply a dot of glue just inside the intersecting lines of one of the corners. Gently press a rosebud onto the glue. In the same manner, work outward to fill each corner box with buds.

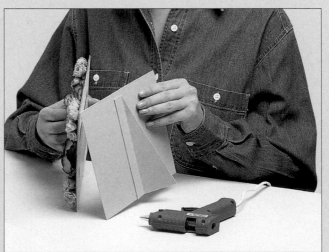

4 Lay rose petals one by one, starting from the outside of the frame and working inward to achieve the desired overlap. Use a single dot of glue for each petal, and be careful to maintain consistency in spacing them.

5 Use the triangular mat piece to make the frame's stand. Lightly score the length of the triangle, about ¾ inch in, and bend it at a right angle to create a tab. Glue the "outside" of the tab and press it to the center of the frame back, so that the broad base of the tripod is flush with the bottom. On the other side of the backing, center the photo, holding it in place with double-sided tape. Lay the floral frame over the photo and adjust, if necessary. Glue the front and back of the frame together at the corners.

# PUNCHED METAL WALL CADDY

*This decorative gift houses tiny valuables in homey style.*

## YOU WILL NEED

- ❏ ¾-INCH-THICK WOOD
- ❏ HANDSAW
- ❏ COPPER SHEET
- ❏ TIN SHEET
- ❏ TIN SNIPS
- ❏ HAMMER & ⅝-INCH NAILS
- ❏ NAIL SET
- ❏ BRASS HOOKS & RINGS
- ❏ RULER

## BEFORE YOU BEGIN

*Working with metal sheeting may initially seem intimidating, but with the right tools and template, you'll be surprised at how easy it can be.*

### Making a Wood Template

Select wood that's at least ¾ inch thick. This provides a strong, sturdy base for the punched tin wall caddy.

**Transfer the house** template (right) to a piece of paper and enlarge it to the desired size of the wall caddy.

**Using the template,** trace the shutter and door designs onto tin; cut out with tin snips.

### Painting Preparation

**Sheets of copper** and tin are available at home supply and craft stores. Sheet metals found at craft stores are better suited for small projects such as these decorative wall caddies.

**To make it easy** to see the pattern lines during cutting, use a grease pencil to mark the design. When finished, wipe the grease from the metal with an all-purpose cleaner.

**Although metal can** be cut with a utility knife, there are various types of snips specifically available for cutting sheet metal. Tin snips are sufficient for cutting straight lines in lightweight sheet metal, but arcs and circles require snips with curved blades.

**When cutting with tin** snips, make the cuts as long as possible. To prevent nicks from resulting, do not close the snips completely.

**After cutting, file away** any sharp edges of the sheet metal with a rough grade of sandpaper.

**To flatten dents** in metal, pound the metal between two pieces of wood.

**To sharpen corner folds** of metal, lightly tap along the fold with a hammer.

**Because brass nails are** soft, use a sharp, steel nail of the same size to begin the nail holes, then replace it with the brass nails.

# Making a Punched Metal Wall Caddy

**1** Transfer template design (Before you Begin) to wood and cut out with handsaw. Sand rough edges smooth and wipe wood clean with damp cloth.

**2** Transfer template to paper, then add 1½ inches at right angles to top, bottom and side edges for folding. Transfer paper template to copper and cut out with tin snips.

**3** Stack wood on top of copper template, then fold copper over sides onto back of wood. Snip extra metal at corners, if necessary, to fold neatly.

## HANDY HINTS

**Use fine steel wool** to buff the surface and give the copper and tin a worn, aged appearance.

**For a tarnished** finish, buff the metals with steel wool, paint over the surface with black latex paint, then wipe off paint with a damp cloth.

**Cover the back of** the wall caddy with heavy felt to keep the metal along the sides from scratching or marring the walls.

**4** Using hammer and ⅝-inch nails, secure copper to back of wood at points and along edges. Be sure to pull copper taut before nailing it into place.

**5** Referring to template for placement, position cut tin shutters and door (Before you Begin) on top of copper. Hold pieces in place with masking tape, if necessary. Nail around edges with ⅝-inch nails.

**6** Using pencil and ruler, lightly draw window details on top of copper. Using nail set, punch circles along pencil marks. It is not necessary to pierce copper.

**7** Using ruler and pencil, measure and mark equal distances along bottom of house for key hooks. Then, measure and mark placement for two rings along slanted roof to hang caddy. Screw in brass hooks and rings so they are facing front. Lightly buff caddy with very fine steel wool to remove any scratches.

# FUN PHOTO CUTOUTS

*Turn favorite photos into unique stand-alone display objects that are fun to give—and receive.*

## YOU WILL NEED

- ❏ PHOTOGRAPH
- ❏ SPRAY ADHESIVE
- ❏ FOAM BOARD
- ❏ MAT KNIFE
- ❏ STRAIGHTEDGE

## BEFORE YOU BEGIN

*Almost any photograph looks fantastic as a cut-out. It's a great way to dramatize an event and showcase happy memories.*

### Choosing a Photograph

**An uninspired background** simply goes away when you cut around the outline of this family pet. Leave the grass in place as the comfortable resting spot.

**Expansive scenes** are all the more dramatic when the outline is emphasized. Cut out the skyline to draw the eye directly to the architectural line of the buildings.

**People are the story.** By eliminating the background, the couple becomes the focal point. Avoid photos with extended arms or fingers, as they are difficult to cut.

### Other Options

- Combine backgrounds and foregrounds of different photographs for dramatic, or sometimes humorous, results.
- Don't be timid about mixing metaphors. A black and white photo comes to life by adding a spot of color to it in the form of a cutout shape mounted on foam board and layered on the photo.
- For a sharp picture, cut out any portion of a photo that may be under- or over-exposed.

# MAKING A PHOTO CUTOUT

1 Place photo facedown on work surface; coat back with adhesive spray. Stick photo onto a piece of foam board; smooth out from center to edges to avoid bubbles.

2 Use a craft knife to cut around edge of image, through all layers. Cut smoothly; do not use a saw-like motion. Make sure white edge of foam board does not show around edges of photo. Keep knife blade pointing straight down or even angle it slightly inward to prevent visibility of the foam board backing.

3 To make an easel stand, cut a 4½- by 3-inch piece of foam board. Score a line ½ inch from one short end; make sure knife goes through top layer of board only, not foam center or bottom board.

4 Apply spray adhesive to back of scored space on easel stand. Stick to back of photo cutout; make sure bottom edge is level with bottom of cutout. Leg will fall back nicely.

# CREATIVELY ETCHED GLASSWARE

*Personalize clear glassware with easy, inexpensive etching. Then give your friends a treasure.*

## YOU WILL NEED

- ❏ GLASS BOWL
- ❏ ETCHING CREAM
- ❏ SELF-ADHESIVE PAPER
- ❏ ARTIST'S TRANSFER PAPER
- ❏ MARKER
- ❏ PENCIL
- ❏ CRAFT KNIFE
- ❏ SPONGE BRUSH
- ❏ RUBBER GLOVES

# BEFORE YOU BEGIN

*Etching is a simple and permanent way to decorate plain glass. Use this technique to create personalized gifts for friends and family.*

## The Basics of Etching

**Etching cream is an acid** that frosts all exposed glass. It can be purchased in craft stores.

**To etch a bowl,** measure its height and circumference; transfer these measurements to graph paper and cut out to form a paper pattern.

**Enlarge the** alphabet template (below) to fit around the bowl. Make any adjustments by enlarging or reducing individual letters. Cut a piece of self-adhesive paper and artist's transfer paper the same size as the graph paper.

**Before applying** the etching cream, rub the contact paper template firmly onto the glass with the back of a spoon. Don't worry about scratching the glass with the blade of the craft knife. The etching will hide the scratches.

## Etching Ideas

- Etch matching salad and soup sets with vegetables and fruits. Reduce the template design for the smaller bowls.
- Create a commemorative cake plate for a special anniversary or birthday.
- Toast the bride and groom with personalized champagne glasses complete with the names and date of the wedding.
- Etch glass tabletops with pretty designs to match the theme of your decor.

# ETCHING GLASSWARE

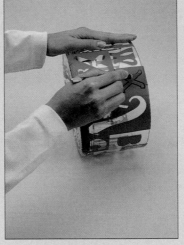

**TAKE NOTE**

**Work in a** well-covered and well-ventilated area and wear protective gloves when working with etching cream. Avoid splattering or dripping the cream and try to work near a source of running water.

**1** Lay self-adhesive paper right side down on flat surface. Lay artist's transfer paper on top of adhesive paper, transfer side facing down, then place template on top. Trace over all lines to transfer letters.

**2** Peel backing off adhesive paper, position around sides of bowl, then carefully press adhesive onto glass. Smooth out wrinkles and bubbles as you go. When adhesive is in place, trace over letters with black marker.

**3** Using a sharp craft knife, cut out inside of all letters to create etching stencil. Keep all edges smooth and straight. To keep from rubbing template design off adhesive, do not allow hands to rest on sides of bowl.

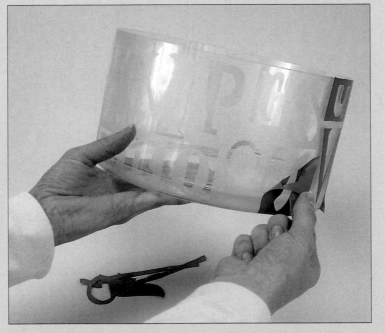

**4** Following manufacturer's instructions, generously apply etching cream to bowl over cut-out letters with sponge brush. Make sure all exposed glass is covered and to keep cream away from skin.

**5** When etching cream has set for required amount of time, rinse bowl thoroughly with cold water. Lift corner of adhesive and remove slowly from bowl, then wash bowl with warm, soapy water.

# Decorated Mailboxes for Indoor Storage

*Fun and whimsical, these mailboxes make wonderful gifts for children.*

## YOU WILL NEED
- ❑ Mailbox
- ❑ Oil-based spray paint
- ❑ Artist's oils in black, white and pink
- ❑ Black grease pencil
- ❑ Permanent marker
- ❑ Polyurethane spray
- ❑ L braces & hardware
- ❑ Drill & level
- ❑ Paper, pencil & ruler
- ❑ Scissors & tape

## BEFORE YOU BEGIN

Mailboxes with animal faces contain and conceal small treasures.

### Box Basics

Set aside the mailbox's metal flag and latch pieces along with all of the necessary hardware.
• Spray paint the entire mailbox, inside and out, with lavender paint. Let the paint dry completely.
• If you prefer brush painting, be sure to choose an oil-based paint for this project.

### Making the Template

**Use the template** (below) to create the cow's face, which will be on the door of the mailbox. First, enlarge the template on a photocopier to achieve the proper size.

Following the outline, use a craft knife to carefully cut out the cow's face, including the nose, ears and horns.

# DECORATING A MAILBOX FOR INDOOR STORAGE

**3** With the black grease pencil, draw freehand outlines of spots randomly around the mailbox. A spot or two can overlap the door slightly without covering the face.

**1** Position the cutout of the cow's face in the center of the mailbox door. Trace around the template with a grease pencil to create a guideline for the rest of the details.

**2** Cut out the shapes of the face and the remaining template. Tape one piece at a time to the door, carefully aligning it with the outline; trace. Repeat until details are complete.

**4** With an artist's brush and black oil paint, fill in the black areas of the face. Fill in the black spots on the rest of the mailbox, too, to mimic the patches of a cow's body.

**5** Let each color of paint dry before applying the next. Paint the cow's nose and ear linings pink. Paint the bow purple and use white paint for the horns and the eyes. Paint the flag (still detached) purple.

**6** After the paint is completely dry, use a permanent black marker to add detailing. Spray the entire box with a protective coat of oil-based polyurethane. Let it dry. Attach the flag and the latch.

## HANDY HINTS

**Upend the mailbox** while spraying with polyurethane to avoid the possibility of the marker lines running.

**Painter's masking** tape holds the pattern pieces securely, but will not leave a mark or remove paint when it is removed.

**7** Locate the wall studs and mark the positions for attaching a pair of sturdy L brackets to the wall for each mailbox to be mounted. Check with a level. Screw the L brackets into the wall.

**8** Set the box on top of the brackets and mark the positions for the screw holes. Put the box on a work surface and bore holes using a drill fitted with a metal bit. Set the mailbox on the brackets and screw into place.

# RIBBON-LACED FRAMES

*These simple plywood frames, softened with ribbon, make charming gifts.*

## YOU WILL NEED

- ❑ ¼-INCH PLYWOOD
- ❑ ½-INCH SATIN RIBBON
- ❑ LATEX PAINT
- ❑ FOAM BRUSH
- ❑ DRILL & ³⁄₁₆-INCH DRILL BIT
- ❑ COPING SAW
- ❑ HEAVY CARDBOARD
- ❑ CARDBOARD EASEL
- ❑ RULER & PENCIL
- ❑ GLUE GUN & GLUE STICKS

## BEFORE YOU BEGIN

*Don't spend hours shopping for the perfect frame. Instead, design your own customized frame from a piece of plywood and decorative ribbon or lacing.*

### Making a Frame Backing

Make the frame backing from black presentation board or any other similar weight board.

• Measure the photo to determine the size of the back opening. Add ⅝ inch to each side and bottom measurement. Add ¼ inch to the top measurement. Cut a piece of board according to the sizes.

• On the backing board, draw a line ⅜ inch from and parallel to the bottom edge. On this line, measure and mark ⅜ inch in from each edge.

• At the top edge, measure and mark ¼ inch from each side. Connect the top and bottom markings to form a "U" shape. Cut along the lines. Save both the outside and inside pieces.

• Center and glue the outer, U-shaped piece to the back of the frame, with the bottom edge positioned ⅝ inch below the frame opening. This provides a groove to hold the backing piece in place.

• Round the bottom edges of the interior piece to make it easier to slide into the U-shaped piece. Then cut a notch in the center of the top edge to make it easier to handle.

• Use spray adhesive or glue stick to secure the photograph to the front of the notched backing piece. Slide it into place on the frame.

• You can purchase a cardboard easel at a craft or art supply store, or you can make one yourself with sturdy cardboard. Check placement and mark carefully to ensure that the frame stands erect. Glue the top edge to the backing piece.

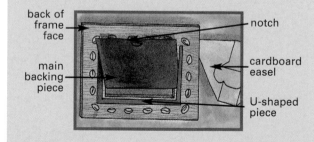

back of frame face — notch

main backing piece — cardboard easel

U-shaped piece

# CONSTRUCTING A LACED FRAME

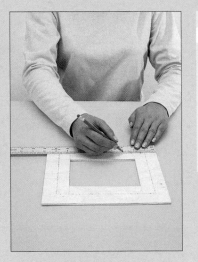

**HANDY HINTS**

**If ribbon frays** during lacing, apply liquid seam protector to ends and let dry. This will prevent unraveling and harden ribbon ends, making it easier to lace.

**1** Add 2 inches all around selected photograph for outside frame dimensions. Cut plywood to outside dimensions. With ruler and pencil, mark opening for picture. Drill one hole just inside markings at one corner.

**2** Insert coping saw blade in drilled hole, reattach blade to saw handle. Saw around all four lines, rounding corners slightly. Once sawing is done, push out center piece. Trim away small pieces left in corners.

**3** With pencil and ruler, mark lines through center of each side. Divide length of line on each side to determine desired number of 3/16-inch-wide holes. Measure and mark hole placements along lines.

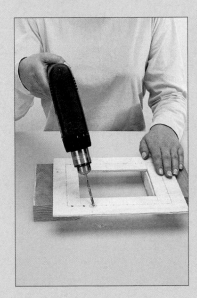

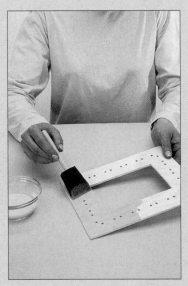

**4** Lift frame by bracing it on two scraps of wood during drilling. Use a new, 3/16-inch drill bit to drill marked holes, one side at a time. Hold drill upright and apply light, even pressure to prevent wood from splintering.

**5** Thin down latex paint with water so that grain of wood remains visible. Erase pencil markings on top side or sand away wood fragments on bottom side. Apply two to three coats of paint to smoother side of frame.

**6** Cut a length of ribbon long enough to weave around frame, plus 2 feet extra for bow. Starting at top center, leave a 12-inch tail and weave ribbon through holes, keeping ribbon smooth between holes. Tie bow at top, trim ends.

# PAINTED FLOWERPOT

*A plain planter livened up with bright splashes of painted color makes a great housewarming gift.*

## BEFORE YOU BEGIN

*Painted designs are the easiest way to give extra life to bland flowerpots. Plan the design carefully to ensure it will fit perfectly around the circumference of the pot.*

### Measuring the Pot

• Draw a pencil line around circumference of pot, 1¾ inches up from bottom. Then measure 1¾ inches down from top and draw another line around circumference. Space between two pencil lines should be 4 inches.

• Draw third line between top and bottom lines to mark center point for diamond shapes.

• There is no need to make other marks for positioning of diamonds and squares, as long as they fit evenly around pot.

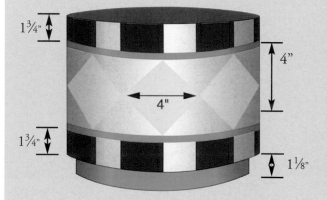

### Painting with a Sponge

Sponge painting produces an interesting, textured effect that perfectly complements the rustic nature of terra-cotta pots.

• Practice first to master sponging technique. A small amount of paint is all that is needed. Dab sponge on paper towel to remove excess paint before applying to surface of pot.

• Use a good-quality sponge. Natural sponges tend to work best, although a regular sink sponge is satisfactory for painting on a clay pot.

• It is essential to use a different sponge for each paint color.

# PAINTING THE POT

3 Use short edge of kitchen sponge to apply green paint along top and bottom lines all around circumference of pot. Allow paint to dry completely. Using same sponge, paint drainage tray green as well.

1 Using white latex paint, sponge entire surface of pot, including 2 inches down inside to cover rim. If necessary, practice on bottom or inside of pot to master sponging technique. Let dry completely.

2 Using measurements given in Before you Begin, mark design lines on pot. Use a pencil and ruler to make marks at correct height around pot, then join marks together to form a continuous line.

### DOLLAR SENSE

**Acrylic paint** is available in small tubes, making it an economical choice for painting small designs. For large pots, it makes financial sense to use latex paint for the undercoat and acrylic paints for the design.

4 Use scissors to cut piece of sponge into a 2¾-inch square. Turn sponge diagonally and use it to paint yellow diamonds between green lines, centering on pencil line. Corners of diamonds should be touching.

5 Cut another piece of sponge into a 1¾-inch square. Use red paint to sponge squares along top and bottom edges of pot. Make sure each red square is centered between two yellow diamonds.

6 Finish design by using the edge of a 1¾-inch kitchen sponge to apply a strip of blue paint down each side of red squares around entire circumference of pot. Allow paint to dry completely. If pot and drainage tray are to be used outdoors, apply one or two coats of clear polyurethane to protect against dirt and moisture.

# Recycled Storage Box

*Use papier-mâché to transform everyday containers into storage gifts worth giving.*

## BEFORE YOU BEGIN

*Believe it or not, that messy craft learned in kindergarten has ancient and honorable origins. Generations of folk artists, along with sophisticated designers, find papier-mâché a wonderfully appealing form of expressive art.*

### Something Old, Something New

**Papier-mâché,** a French term that has passed into the English language unchanged, is the craft of fashioning inexpensive, lightweight objects from "mashed paper." Its origins trace to the invention of paper in ancient China, where warriors' masks were among the first items made.

**Refinements**—the use of lacquers to harden and strengthen the material—came to Europe in the 17th century and have been in popular and productive use ever since.

**Preparation** for making papier-mâché objects begins with tearing the newspaper.

**Tearing** is the key to achieving feathered edges and this in turn produces a smoother surface later when layer upon layer of paper strips are built up. Using a steel rule as an edge, tear rather than cut paper into strips approximately 3 by 12 inches.

**Shredded paper** is a more expensive alternative. Sold in hobby stores as dried ground pulp, it can be mixed with water and a filler to get a clay-like consistency. This material is best used in making figurines and other irregular shapes.

**Once the paper is torn,** mix equal parts of flour and water in a bowl to use as a paste.

### Container Prep

- All sorts of throw-away containers make suitable underpinnings for recycling projects. The chief requirement is that their size be right for the intended storage task and that they be sufficiently sturdy to withstand several coats of wet newspapers.
- Check boxes at corners before beginning and add reinforcing tape inside, if necessary. Remove or sand rough wood burrs on boxes and baskets.

# DECORATING A BOX

1 Mix one part flour with one part water to a consistency of runny cake batter. Pour the mixture to cover the bottom of a pan. Lay in a paper strip and brush its upper side. Turn the strip over, brush to coat again.

2 Drape strips of wet paper one by one over the insides and outsides of a clean, smooth wooden box. Smooth in place with the brush. When the surfaces are covered, repeat the process six to eight times.

3 Allow the box to dry completely. Depending upon the number of paper layers and atmospheric conditions, this can take as long as 48 hours. When the project is dry, apply two base coats of latex paint.

4 Lightly pencil in all the elements of the design. Though you are aiming for a fairly free expression of curving lines and accent spots, it is still important to maintain some consistency in the repeats.

5 Apply the design, starting with the wavy line. To avoid smearing, allow each colorway to dry thoroughly before applying the next. For a durable top coat, apply a final application of polyurethane. This will intensify colors while waterproofing the surfaces.

# Foam Rubber Picture Mats

*Showcase special pictures in lighthearted, colorful mats, then give them to special people.*

## YOU WILL NEED

❏ THIN SHEETS OF FOAM RUBBER
❏ SCISSORS & CRAFT KNIFE
❏ METAL STRAIGHTEDGE
❏ CRAFT GLUE
❏ CARDBOARD
❏ PHOTOGRAPH
❏ FLAT MAGNETS
❏ PENCIL

## BEFORE YOU BEGIN

*Framing photos with colorful foam rubber shapes is a great project for kids. Let them pick their favorite shots and help them cut the foam. It's that easy!*

### Keeping it Simple

• Begin with simple shapes until you feel comfortable with the flexibility of the foam rubber. If children are involved in creating the project, very simple shapes like circles or squares can be cut easily with children's scissors.

• Foam rubber, in sheets about ⅛-inch-thick, is available in a wide variety of colors. Refer to the picture being framed to help select the color for the mat. Hold the picture next to different colors of mat and select a color combination that gives the frame a strong graphic appeal.

• Decorative mats look great alone, but can be framed to add another dimension to the composition. Choose simple frames that do not detract from the mats. Remove the glass.

### Using Templates

**Draw your own shapes** on graph paper or use cookie cutters as templates for simple designs. To use the templates provided here, enlarge them with a photocopier until they are the desired size. Or enlarge by using a grid and graph paper.

**Trace the shapes** onto cardboard for templates that can be used more than once.

# MAKING A FOAM RUBBER MAT

**1** To make a template for a tree-shaped mat, make a photocopy to the right size or use graph paper to draw it to scale. Use scissors to carefully cut out the whole tree shape—the trunk and the leaves.

**2** Trace the whole tree onto thin cardboard for a template. Use a craft knife to cut out the cardboard, cutting ⅛ inch within the outline, to create a backing for the mat. Trace the tree again onto a second piece of cardboard.

**3** Cut the tree template into two pieces, and trace them onto foam rubber—brown for the trunk, green for the leaves. Use scissors to cut out the leaves and a craft knife to cut the tree trunk and picture window.

### TAKE NOTE

**When cutting** the picture window, take care that the knife does not cut too far into the corners. Begin cutting at each corner and work toward the center on each side.

**Keep a careful eye** on children, and make sure they use child-safe scissors at all times.

### DOLLAR SENSE

**To protect** a favorite photo, glue a sheet of clear plastic over the front of the picture. This is an excellent alternative to heavy picture glass.

**4** Cut the photograph to the desired size; glue it in position on the cardboard backing. Then glue the rubber trunk and leaves in position on the cardboard. Take care the glue doesn't seep out the sides.

**5** When the glue is completely dry, turn the mat facedown and use glue to attach a small magnet to the back. Repeat this procedure to create different-shaped mats such as a star, house, sun and evergreen tree. Kids will love to use the mats to mount photos of favorite celebrities on a school locker, while adults will put them to good use framing family snapshots to decorate a refrigerator or bulletin board.

# GIFTS WITH
# PLANTS &
# FLOWERS

*The colors and fragrances of nature enhance any gift idea, any season of the year. So here are dozens of ways to put plants and flowers to good work when it's time to create gifts of importance. You'll find a wide variety of ideas for wreaths, arrangements for seasonal fresh flowers, instructions on how to dry flowers and create bouquets from them, creative concepts for holding your displays, and much more. When it's time to create gifts, don't forget about plants and flowers, and the natural touch of subtle beauty they bring to any creation.*

# COUNTRY CLASSIC GRAPEVINE WREATH

*This woodsy wreath is a charming gift for use on anyone's wall.*

## YOU WILL NEED

- ❑ GRAPEVINE WREATH
- ❑ HONEYSUCKLE VINE
- ❑ DRIED PODS
- ❑ PINECONES
- ❑ DRIED PHALARIS GRASS
- ❑ DRIED HYDRANGEA
- ❑ FLORIST'S WIRE
- ❑ GLUE GUN & GLUE STICKS
- ❑ SCISSORS

## BEFORE YOU BEGIN

*A wide variety of dried flowers, pods and grasses are available at most florist's shops and craft stores. But they can also be collected from nature—even from your own backyard.*

### Collecting Flowers and Plants

Cones, pods and grasses are natural finds outdoors.
• Collect them after they have fallen to the ground or take them from trees.
• Wild grasses can be snipped at leisure, so travel with scissors on nature walks.
• It's not worth the effort to make your own grapevine wreaths; buy them pre-made at flower or craft stores instead.

### Preparing Flowers and Plants

**Lay wild grasses** flat along the bottom of a cardboard box lined with newspaper; allow to dry. Turn the grasses over occasionally to ensure even drying.

**Hydrangea is best dried** upright with water. Pour water into vase to depth of 2 inches. Place the flowers upright in vase; allow to dry. Water evaporates, leaving flowers preserved.

**Wheat and other grains** should be dried upside down. Bundle the stalks together loosely and secure near the ends of the stems with a rubber band or twine. Hang to dry.

# DECORATING THE WREATH

1 Position honeysuckle vine on the wreath. Take florist's wire, attached to the spool, and wrap around wreath to attach the vine. Continue until desired look is achieved. Cut wire and twist ends behind the wreath.

2 Apply glue to the back of a pod and position on the wreath. Hold in place until firmly attached. Repeat with a variety of dried pods and pinecones, gluing them on in clusters of three or four.

3 Cut down the stems of the phalaris grass to about 2 inches long. Gather into groups of two or three and apply glue to the ends. Place in among the clusters of pods and cones, holding until glue sets.

**TAKE NOTE**

Wreaths decorated with dried and preserved materials are fragile and can break and fade. To make them last longer, keep them out of direct sunlight, away from humid conditions, and move them as little as possible.

**OOPS**

If flowers or grasses break or fall off the wreath, simply replace them with new ones. This is a great way to add new colors and shapes to change the look of the wreath.

4 Glue the stem of a dried hydrangea floret and position on wreath. Continue adding hydrangea florets to surround the pod clusters and fill in empty spaces. Tuck in loose honeysuckle vines.

# DRIED-FLOWER WALL BASKET

*Artfully arranged dried flowers add color and cheer to any wall.*

## BEFORE YOU BEGIN

*Easily transform a plain basket or container into an integral part of a dried floral display by covering it with green sphagnum moss.*

### Decorating the Basket with Moss

- Begin with a basket made from plastic, wood or wire. It need not look perfect since it will soon be covered completely with moss.
- Use a hot glue gun to attach moss quickly, easily and permanently to the holder.
- Sphagnum moss is invaluable as a cover or base for many types of dried and fresh floral arrangements. If the moss is fresh, let it air-dry in a basket or box before beginning.
- Gather a generous clump of moss. With a glue gun, apply glue to the back of the clump and then position the moss on the outside of the basket.

- Working in one direction, glue pieces of moss to cover holder completely. Position moss next to—not overlapping—previous clump to ensure a smooth base.

- Remember to cover rim so no part of basket remains visible.
- In order for the basket to hang on the wall, it must have a flat back. If it does not already have a hook or loop for hanging, make one with wire or raffia and attach it to the back.

### Flower Care

Take special care to ensure your arrangement lasts a long time.
- Avoid a location that is exposed to continuous sunlight and/or moisture.
- Dust periodically with a soft paintbrush. Sturdy arrangements can be dusted with a hair dryer set on a low, cold setting.
- When it is not on display, store the arrangement in a loose paper bag in a dry location.

# ARRANGING THE FLOWERS

**HANDY HINTS**

**Dried hydrangea** flower heads are quite fragile, so handle them with care. To store unused dried hydrangeas, wrap each head individually in soft tissue paper.

**Since long stems** tend to look bare once they have dried and lost their leaves, fill in the stem area with shorter flower heads.

1 Cut a block of florist's foam to fit inside basket. Use hot glue to secure foam to bottom of basket. It may be necessary to use a serrated knife to carve bottom of block so that it sits securely in bottom of basket.

2 Begin by sticking single stems of wild oats all around back and sides of foam. Position stems evenly so arrangement looks balanced, taking care that tops are not bunched too closely together.

3 Position shorter stems of wild oats in front of first batch, working from back of arrangement toward front. Add additional dried flowers for color and texture. Make sure arrangement is well balanced.

4 Complete arrangement with dried hydrangea blossoms. Use them to fill in gaps at front in lower part of display. They will give the arrangement a very full appearance.

# COLORFUL FLOWERS FOR SPRING

*Arrange flowers of vivid colors to form a dazzling spring still life that will brighten anyone's day ... and week!*

## BEFORE YOU BEGIN

*Trim the flowers, seal the ends, then choose a spiky frog to hold your display. Short and squat or tall and trim, there's a frog for every arrangement.*

### Preparing the Flowers

Daffodils require a little special care and preparation before they can be used in an arrangement.
• Remove any foliage that will be below the waterline in the arrangement.
• Sap from the stems of the daffodils can poison the water and the other flowers used in the arrangement. To prevent this, dip the ends of the daffodil stems in boiling water for about 20 seconds to seal the ends. Alternatively, hold the stem ends over the flame of a candle.

### Choosing the Frog

**This needlepoint frog** has pins at the base that fit together to form either a square, a circle or an oblong shape. Each piece can be used individually for smaller flower arrangements as well. Other frogs do not interconnect, but come in a range of sizes. Spiky frogs normally hold flowers straight up and down.

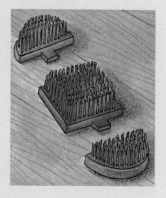

**Round, green hairpin** frogs have heavy lead bases and flexible brass wires to hold the stalky stems of spring-flowering bulbs and flowers at any angle—including a straight up and down position. Another advantage of hairpin frogs is there are no sharp points to prick your fingers.

# ARRANGING THE FLOWERS

**HANDY HINTS**

**Press flower stems** gently but firmly into the spiky frog. If one of the stems breaks, just cut above the break and reposition in the arrangement.

**TAKE NOTE**

**Display** arrangement in a cool location, out of direct sunlight. Avoid excessively hot or cold areas.

1 Place the spiky frog in the bottom of the teacup. If the frog is not weighty enough to hold flowers upright, put some florist's clay in the bottom of the teacup and press the frog onto it to hold in place.

2 Begin by cutting the mini daffodils to various lengths. The longest stems should be three times the teacup height. Insert the longer stems in the center of the frog and the shorter ones around the sides.

3 Trim the stems of the allium to about twice the height of the teacup. Press the stems firmly into the spiky frog around the sides of the arrangement to produce a layered effect.

5 Stand back and view the arrangement from all sides. Fill any sparse or bare spaces with extra daffodils, allium or grape hyacinths. Then add floral preservative to lukewarm water and fill the teacup.

4 After cutting the stems of the grape hyacinths to two or three times the teacup height, push them into the spiky frog, longer stems closer to the center and shorter stems to fill out the sides.

# KITCHEN HERBS IN BASKETS

*These fragrant and functional herb baskets make great little gardens ... and great little gifts.*

## YOU WILL NEED

- ❑ SMALL BASKETS FOR HANGING
- ❑ SCISSORS
- ❑ HEAVY CLEAR PLASTIC
- ❑ DRAINAGE MATERIAL
- ❑ STARTER HERBS
- ❑ POTTING SOIL

# BEFORE YOU BEGIN

*Some herbs are perfect for flavoring teas, while others are potent enough for vinegar. Use herbs to season butter, or simply snip and add to any dish.*

## Using Herbs

### Tea

**Lemon balm** Boil dried leaves in water and strain for a lemony tea

**Chamomile** Steep whole dried flowers in hot water for an apple-flavored tea

**Mint** Dry leaves and steep in hot water for a light, refreshing tea

### Vinegar

**Basil** Add to vinegar and leave 5-6 weeks for a pungent flavor

**Oregano** Long sprigs of fresh leaves add robust Italian flavor

**Rosemary** Use whole, fresh leaves for a spicy vinegar dressing

### Butter

**Sage** Dry leaves and crumble into softened butter for poultry

**Dill** Add fresh dill leaves to butter for a unique taste with fish

**Coriander** Seeds add sweet, slightly pungent flavor to butter on bread

### Seasoning

**Bay** Use fresh or dried leaves in sauces, soups and stews

**Chives** Snip fresh, grass-like stems for a mild onion flavor

**Thyme** Dried or fresh, a perfect accent for fresh vegetables

# PLANTING THE HERBS

1 Cut a piece of heavy clear plastic to roughly the same size as the basket, then line the inside of the basket. If the plastic does not cling to the sides of the basket, use double-sided tape to secure.

2 Place a layer of drainage material (broken pieces of a clay pot or small stones) in the bottom of the lined basket. This protective layer keeps the roots of the herbs from standing in water and getting soggy.

3 Run a knife around inside edge of the starter plant containers and gently squeeze containers to loosen soil. Then tip containers and carefully remove plants. If soil isn't loose enough, add water to moisten.

## HANDY HINTS

**Water the herbs** when the top ½ inch of soil is dry. Letting the soil dry between waterings is good for the plants and makes for easy care. Mist herbs once a week to keep leaves fresh.

## TAKE NOTE

**Feed plants** with a diluted all-purpose houseplant food every two months—or not at all. Herbs tend to lose their flavor if they are fertilized too much.

## HERBS FOR BASKETS

TALL PLANTS FOR THE LARGE BASKET

❑ BASIL AND JAPANESE BASIL
❑ CHIVES
❑ ITALIAN AND CURLY PARSLEY

## PLANTS FOR LARGE & HANGING BASKETS

❑ OREGANO
❑ ROSEMARY
❑ SAGE
❑ TARRAGON
❑ THYME AND LEMON THYME

4 Gently place two or three of the starter plants in the center of the basket. Loosely add potting soil around the plants to fill in the basket. Water the plants, and then hang the basket in a window that gets full sun.

# FLOWER-FILLED POTS

*Add beautiful dried flowers to simple clay pots for gifts with a rustic, country feel.*

## YOU WILL NEED

- ❏ TERRA-COTTA POTS
- ❏ DRIED FLOWERS
- ❏ SHEET MOSS
- ❏ FLORIST'S FOAM
- ❏ SERRATED KNIFE
- ❏ GLUE GUN & GLUE STICK

## BEFORE YOU BEGIN

*A simple terra-cotta pot makes the perfect starting point for a variety of different floral displays. The pot itself can be decorated easily to enhance the dried flowers inside.*

### Decorating Terra-Cotta Pots

**Begin with a new pot** or simply clean an old pot with disinfectant. Allow the pot to dry thoroughly before painting. For a slightly aged appearance, paint a base coat of acrylic paint on the outside of the pot.

**Before the paint dries** completely, use a bunched-up clean cotton rag to rub gently around the surface of the pot. Continue to rub in a variety of directions to create texture. Re-bunch the rag periodically.

**Sponging adds a mottled** effect and is easy to do. Simply dip a small piece of sponge into paint and dab it onto the pot. Natural sea sponges are the easiest to use and have the right texture and paint absorbency.

**Add a stenciled design** to the pot for a pretty, country appeal. The stencil can be used on a plain or painted pot. Be sure that the stencil material is flexible enough to bend to the shape of the pot.

# ARRANGING THE FLOWERS

1 Use serrated knife to cut plastic foam to shape of pot; leave a 1-inch gap below top of pot. If necessary, apply a dab of hot glue inside base of pot to hold plastic foam in place.

2 Pull sheet moss into 6-inch pieces. Use hot glue to attach moss pieces around top of pot and 2 inches down sides. Attach a thin covering of moss over entire top of pot.

4 Use hot glue to fill in spaces with smaller, stemless flowers and leaves. Make sure top of pot is completely covered and take care that colors are evenly distributed.

3 Lay out all flowers on work surface, with like varieties grouped together. Choose flowers and colors that work well together as a group. First select larger flowers with stems; push stems into plastic foam. Position different flowers all around pot; do not clump similar flowers in one area.

# LINEN AND SILK WREATH

*Combine silk flowers and delicate linens for an everlasting wreath that can become a meaningful gift.*

## YOU WILL NEED

- ❏ 14-INCH STRAW WREATH
- ❏ THREE 6-OUNCE BAGS OF RAFFIA
- ❏ SILK FLOWERS
- ❏ HANDKERCHIEFS OR LINENS
- ❏ FLORAL PINS
- ❏ GLUE GUN
- ❏ RIBBON
- ❏ FLORIST'S WIRE

## BEFORE YOU BEGIN

*Accent your wreath with linens—use either newly purchased table linens and antique handkerchiefs —or tea dye some new items to make them look antique.*

### Tea Dyeing Linens

**These illustrations show** the subtle colors produced by tea dyeing white linen for 5 minutes (below left) and for 30 minutes (below right).

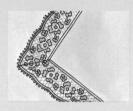 

### Making the Linen Flowers

**Pull the linen** square up from its center and gather in your hands. Wrap gathered section with thread or florist's wire several times to create a flower blossom.

### Planning the Wreath

**A balanced wreath** has its decorative elements distributed evenly around the wreath.

**A grouped wreath** has its elements clustered into separate groups.

A combination wreath, such as the wreath in the photograph at left, has randomly distributed groupings of flowers and linens that use a variety of colors.

# MAKING THE WREATH

1 Straighten raffia; loop one end. Wrap raffia onto straw base with a spool of florist's wire. Continue looping and wrapping raffia; do not cut wire until whole wreath is wrapped. Secure wire behind wreath.

2 Use Before you Begin as a reference for positioning flowers and linens. Attach silk hydrangea leaves to base using florist's pins. Do not completely cover base with leaves.

3 Position linen flowers between silk leaves; pin into place with florist's pins. Pin hydrangea blooms and peonies around wreath at desired positions.

### HANDY HINTS

**To prevent fading,** spray flowers with a clear acrylic UV guard, available at craft stores. If fading has already occurred, lightly spray blooms with colored spray paint made for flowers.

### TAKE NOTE

**Do not** cut the plastic covering or the strings from the straw base—they help to hold the straw together.

4 Smaller silk flowers must be glued onto wreath. Apply hot glue to flower and then press firmly onto wreath. Hold each flower in place for about 20 seconds to ensure glue has adhered to it.

5 Weave ribbon around silk flowers. French wired ribbon works best because it holds whatever shape it is given. Place small dots of hot glue on ribbon when it is in desired position and attach to base. Tuck ribbon ends under flowers or raffia. Once wreath is complete, determine which way to hang it. Create a loop from florist's wire and attach it securely to straw base.

# DECORATIVE PLANTERS WITH MOLDING

*Use simple moldings to turn a plain planter into a showpiece—a great gift for someone who appreciates container gardening.*

## YOU WILL NEED

- ❏ PLANTER
- ❏ 2¼-INCH CROWN MOLDING
- ❏ 2-INCH BASE MOLDING
- ❏ ½ x 5½-INCH CLEAR PINE
- ❏ TAPE MEASURE
- ❏ MITER BOX & SAW
- ❏ CONSTRUCTION ADHESIVE
- ❏ NO. 8 FINISHING NAILS
- ❏ EXTERIOR WOOD SEALER
- ❏ PAINT & PAINTBRUSH
- ❏ POLYURETHANE
- ❏ WOOD FINISHING STAIN

## BEFORE YOU BEGIN

*Moldings and decorative motifs add texture and design interest to a plain planter. Embellish wood, plaster, pottery and plastic planters with attractive trim.*

### Shopping for Decorative Trim

**The variety of** molding styles is tremendous. They are often made from oak, which can be stained, or poplar, which should be painted.

### Molding and Motif Styles

**Intricate carvings** such as leaf patterns, grapevines and flowers are elegant, while simpler rope-twist borders, sugar-twist beading and linear carvings look smart on plain surfaces.

**Motifs, whether embossed** or carved, can be used alone or grouped. Single motifs, such as swags and medallions, should be large enough to balance and fill space. Grouped motifs take many forms, from florals suitable for clustering to corner motifs that enhance planter edges.

**Molding strips** are available in a multitude of styles in lengths of 6 to 16 feet. Alternatively, look for kits that have cut lengths of molding with the edges already mitered.

### Molding Tips

- Home improvement stores and lumberyards are the best sources for moldings and motifs. Many will even sell remnants at a discount.
- The adhesive must be compatible with the material from which the planter is made. Check with a home improvement store for advice.
- Make sure the molding design will break attractively at the corners of the planter.

# ADDING DECORATIVE MOLDING

**HANDY HINTS**

**Some moldings** are sold with miter guides that make it simple and fool-proof to cut accurate joints. If there is no miter guide, remember to keep the decorative edge to the outside when cutting the miter.

1 Measure sides of planter, adding extra length for corner miters. Use miter box and saw to cut base molding, crown molding and clear pine to desired length. Sand rough spots on cut edges.

2 Apply construction adhesive to back of one crown molding strip; press molding in place around top edges of planter. Repeat with remaining crown molding. Wipe away extra adhesive from joints.

3 Use construction adhesive to attach base molding around bottom of planter and clear pine on top of crown molding around rim. Allow adhesive to dry. Secure strips with No. 8 finishing nails.

5 Stain body of planter with any commercial finishing stain or tinted water sealer. Allow to dry, then apply second coat. Apply one or two coats of polyurethane to inside and outside of planter to seal.

4 Prime molding and clear pine with exterior wood sealer. Allow to dry for 24 hours, then paint molding and clear pine with desired color. Apply second coat of paint when first coat has dried. Seal with one or two coats of polyurethane.

# MINIATURE FLOWERING BOX GARDENS

*Bring the gift of the outdoors inside with these mini versions of summer gardens.*

## BEFORE YOU BEGIN

*Before planting your mini garden, take these preparatory steps to prevent the box from becoming stained or damaged.*

### Preparing the Box

**Choose a sturdy box** with a solid bottom. Make sure the sides meet squarely at the corners so that water and soil don't leak out. Check the outside of the box for nails, splinters and other potentially dangerous protrusions.

**Consider lining** the sides and bottom of the box with moss, dead leaves or other dried natural materials if you are concerned that the plastic will show through. This will also provide an additional barrier against moisture.

**Using a paintbrush,** paint the inside of the box with wood sealant or waterproof varnish (below); let dry. For

extra protection, paint the outside of the box as well. If you prefer a bright, colorful box instead of one with a natural finish, substitute waterproof paint for the varnish.

**To protect the box** from moisture and the surface on which it is placed from leakage, lay a plastic trash bag over the box and press it flat on the bottom and into the side (above). Let the edges hang over the top of the box.

### Which Box?

• Wooden planters made from aged wood with a natural finish create a rustic look. Shipping crates, wine boxes and durable fruit baskets with solid bottoms also have rustic appeal.

• Plastic boxes with deep sides are colorful and contemporary.
• Strong wicker baskets will also work well. Be sure to hide the plastic liner with moss or dead leaves.

# PLANTING THE BOX

**HANDY HINTS**

**In darker rooms,** use mini box gardens as colorful, decorative accessories for special occasions. But move them to sunnier spots for everyday storage.

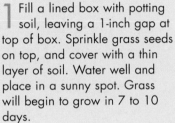

1 Fill a lined box with potting soil, leaving a 1-inch gap at top of box. Sprinkle grass seeds on top, and cover with a thin layer of soil. Water well and place in a sunny spot. Grass will begin to grow in 7 to 10 days.

2 Once grass has grown to at least 4 inches long, use liner to help you remove it from box in one clump. Working on top of liner, gently separate grass into smaller clumps using fingers or a butter knife.

3 Line planter with fresh plastic and fill with soil to within 1 inch of top. Dig a hole in middle of soil and add a seasonal flowering plant. Gently dig holes around plant, being careful not to damage roots; add small clumps of grass. Carefully pat down soil around plant and grass to secure.

4 Once plants are pleasingly arranged in planter, use scissors to cut liner so that it is level with top of box. Place box on a table or windowsill that receives appropriate amount of light for flowering plant. Water regularly; feed during spring and summer months. If grass grows too long, use a sharp pair of scissors to trim it to desired length. Properly cared for, box garden should last indefinitely.

# BEAUTIFUL HANGING FLORAL SPHERE

*A hanging floral centerpiece makes a beautiful, unique gift.*

## YOU WILL NEED
- ❏ FLORIST'S FOAM
- ❏ FRESH YEW & BOXWOOD
- ❏ FRESH FREESIA, LILY, POM-POM, GERBERA, DELPHINIUM, SPRAY ROSE, STOCK & QUEEN ANNE'S LACE
- ❏ CHICKEN WIRE
- ❏ FLORIST'S WIRE
- ❏ RIBBON
- ❏ SERRATED KNIFE
- ❏ WIRE CUTTER

## BEFORE YOU BEGIN

*To make a hanging floral sphere with fresh flowers and greens, simply choose materials that are in season.*

### Spring and Summer

- Star magnolia is an elegant white flower with a sweet aroma.
- Carnations come in red, white, pink or yellow and are long-lasting.
- Peony is fragrant with a large, silky flower head and can be found in red, white, yellow or pink.
- Cornflower is generally a vibrant blue, but is also available in white, pink, mauve and red.

### Autumn and Winter

- Poinsettia is known as the Christmas flower because of its large, red bracts and dark green leaves. It is also found with white, pink or variegated bracts.
- Boxwood is an evergreen with dark green or variegated, shiny leaves.
- Sunflower has large, yellow, daisy-like petals.
- Chrysanthemum features a "button" center with radiating petals. Traditional colors are warm orange, yellow, lavender and pink.

# MAKING A FLORAL SPHERE

**HANDY HINTS**

**Add dimension** to the display by making two different-sized spheres.

**For a contemporary** look, create hanging spheres featuring flowers in shades of the same color. For example, strong shades of yellow are ideal for the sun-filled days of spring.

1 Use serrated knife to cut 4- to 6-inch square block of florist's foam. Shave off corners of foam to form more rounded shape. Soak foam in bucket of cold water overnight or until completely saturated.

2 Cut piece of chicken wire large enough to fit around foam. Wrap wire around foam and tuck ends together to secure in place. Make sure wire is pressed flat against foam and no rough angles protrude.

3 Cut length of ribbon long enough to hang finished sphere and tie onto top of sphere. Loop one ribbon end through chicken wire and secure with florist's wire. Test to make sure it will hold.

5 Push flowers into foam until sphere is completely covered. Adjust stem lengths to form round, even shape. Use smallest flowers to fill gaps. Use florist's wire to attach large bow to top of completed sphere. Keep foam moist to prolong life of flowers.

4 Hang sphere so flowers can be arranged without damaging blossoms on opposite side. Trim greens and flowers to 4-inch lengths. Cover sphere loosely and randomly with greens, pushing stems into foam so they extend no more than 1 inch.

# NATURAL SEASHELL WREATH

*Create a shell-adorned wreath for a fun, nautical gift.*

## BEFORE YOU BEGIN

*Gather an assortment of shells on your next trip to the beach. Then glue them to a twig-based wreath for a wonderful, decorative way to bring the seashore home or to someone special.*

### Preparing the Shells

**Shells in their** natural state are unique in coloration, size and shape. Use a good mix of shells on your wreath to make the display as interesting as possible.

**When gathering shells,** be sure they are no longer a home for living sea creatures. If there is a persistent odor, the shell may still be harboring the remains of an animal. In that case, boil the shell in water for several minutes.

**Paint shells for a different** look. Their texture makes them perfect for gilding with gold spray paint or decorating with acrylic paints.

**To prepare shells,** wash them in a basin filled with warm, soapy water. Line the basin with a towel to prevent breaking or damaging the delicate edges of the shells.

**To protect and add shine** to shells, spray them with clear polyurethane (below). Allow one side to dry completely before spraying the other side.

### Using Twigs

Collect twigs on your travels to be used in wreaths at a later date:
• Cut twigs in winter when the sap is low.
• To dry twigs, lay them flat on an absorbent surface in a cool, dry place. Make sure the twigs are well spaced, so that air can circulate around them.
• For a really rustic look, try to find twigs that still have small pinecones in place.

# MAKING A SEASHELL WREATH

**HANDY HINTS**

**Florist and specialty** shops sell beautiful shells to use in wreaths. However, it is more fun and more cost effective to gather your own shells from the beach. To give shells a still-wet appearance, cover them with a thin coat of varnish. To make it easy to reach all sides of the shell, hammer a nail into a block of wood and then use a small piece of tacky adhesive to fix the shell on top. Remove the shell when it is completely dry.

**1** Arrange twigs in bunches. Insert first bunch into metal clamps of wreath frame. Continue adding bunches until frame is covered. Make sure all bunches overlap slightly and point in same direction.

**2** Gather together several strands of bear grass and wire them into a loop. Hot-glue loops all around wreath. Glue clusters of dried sea grapes or other dried foliage between bear grass loops.

**3** Glue shells all around wreath. If shell is heavy or awkwardly shaped, wire it to base and then add a dab of glue for security. Add more shells or bear grass as necessary to fill in gaps and balance wreath.

**4** Spray entire wreath with clear polyurethane to give it shine and protect it from dust. Shellac or hair spray can also be used as a protective spray. Attach a strong loop of raffia to back of wreath to hold it securely in place on wall.

# FRESH FLOWERS IN LITTLE BASKETS

*Give a floral arrangement in a little basket to make a colorful impact.*

## BEFORE YOU BEGIN

*Taking a few steps to prepare foliage and flowers will help create a longer-lasting and more attractive arrangement.*

### Preparing Flowers and Foliage

**All stems should** be recut on the diagonal. This will expose the greatest amount of stem area, allowing the flower to absorb more water. Remove the lower leaves and thorns from the part of each stem that will be inserted into the floral foam. Otherwise, the leaves will rot and contaminate the arrangement.

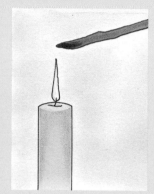

**For sturdy green** and woody stems such as azalea, camellia and eucalyptus, scrape the bottom 2 inches of bark from the stem. Using sharp florist's scissors, cut from the base of the stem upward 2 inches; then cut the slit stem diagonally. This helps the stem absorb water faster.

**For milky stems,** including poppies and ferns, seal the stem to extend the life of the flower. Carefully singe the cut end of the stem with a match or candle flame until it turns black (above right). This forces the sap to rise, but still allows the water to enter the stem.

### A Quick Lift

**If the floral material** starts to look a little droopy, revive it prior to arranging. To revive most types of foliage and some flowers, totally submerge them in a bucket filled with cool water (left) or run them under the tap for about five minutes. For large stems, use a bathtub. Be sure to soak all treated stems upright in a bucket of cool water for several hours before arranging them.

# MAKING THE ARRANGEMENT

1 Line each basket with a piece of cellophane. Soak floral foam in water. Cut the floral foam to fit comfortably in the basket and place within the cellophane. Fill the basket halfway with water.

2 Prepare greens and flowers (Before you Begin). Insert greens into foam to lightly cover the entire exposed area. Beginning with poppy, intermittently insert the stems into the floral foam.

3 Follow the shape of the container and arrange flowers so that each type is evenly distributed around the arrangement. Always begin with the largest flower head and finish with smallest blossoms.

4 Once the largest flowers are evenly displayed, fill in with solidaster and additional greens to round out and fill up the entire basket. Check the arrangement for any gaps or holes and fill in. It is usually easiest to work with one type of flower at a time.

# FLORAL AND VEGETABLE ARRANGEMENT

*Celebrate nature's bounty with a floral and vegetable centerpiece.*

## YOU WILL NEED

❏ FRUITS & VEGETABLES
❏ FOLIAGE & FLOWERS
❏ FLORIST'S FOAM
❏ WOODEN FLORAL PICKS
❏ DECORATIVE BASKET
❏ PLASTIC LINER
❏ SCISSORS

## BEFORE YOU BEGIN

*When creating an arrangement, choose flowers and vegetables with similar life spans.*

### Natural Selection

Vegetables will remain fresh for time spans ranging from a few days to a couple of weeks. It is best to choose vegetables that are very firm. Keep them refrigerated if they are not used upon picking or purchasing. Also, keep the arrangement out of direct sunlight.

### Selecting Vegetables

| Vegetable | Color | Life Expectancy |
|---|---|---|
| Asparagus | green | 2-3 days |
| Potatoes | red or brown | 1-2 weeks |
| Artichoke | green | 5 days |
| Eggplant | purple | 5-7 days |
| Bell Peppers | yellow, red, green | 1-2 weeks |
| Squash | yellow, green, orange | 5 days |
| Turnips | pink and white | 3 weeks |
| Mushrooms | brown, white | 3 days |

### Preserving Natural Materials

Once the vegetables have been picked, they can be preserved to last longer than their natural life expectancy.
• Glycerin and clear acrylic floor wax are two quick and easy ways to preserve natural materials.
• Dip vegetables in clear acrylic floor wax, let dry on wax paper, then apply two more coats of wax. The wax seals the skins, extending the life span.
• Preserve leaves in a variety of colors by soaking the stems in equal parts of boiling water and glycerin (available in most drugstores). Crush the ends of the stems to help them absorb the mixture.

# ARRANGING A FLORAL AND VEGETABLE BASKET

## HANDY HINTS

**For a long-lasting** arrangement, consider substituting quality latex fruits and vegetables for natural materials. Enhance the display with fresh foliage and flowers.

**Disguise bruised** marks on fruits and vegetables by turning them bruised side down and piercing them with a floral pick.

1 Place a large block of florist's foam inside the plastic liner of a wicker basket. Soak the foam with water, being careful to keep water inside the plastic liner. If necessary, drain excess water from the liner.

2 Poke a floral pick through the bottom of each vegetable, leaving half of the pick exposed. If possible, position the pick so that it punctures through the meat of the vegetable for a sturdy hold.

3 Working from the center of the basket and moving outward, position the large vegetables firmly in the foam on angles. Fill in gaps with smaller vegetables.

## TAKE NOTE

**When preserving** natural materials, use a hair dryer to speed the process. Otherwise, it can take up to a week for some naturals to dry.

5 Using scissors, cut the ends of the flower stems on a diagonal. Complete the arrangement by filling in any gaps with assorted cut flowers and foliage, mixing colors to create pretty contrasts. Choose flowers that last as long as the vegetables.

4 Using scissors, cut the end of each leaf stem on a diagonal. Beginning on one side of the basket, poke each leaf stem into the florist's foam. Layer the foliage underneath the fruit, balancing the display.

# HARVEST FRUIT WREATHS

*Use colorful fruit to create these gifts that look good enough to eat.*

## You Will Need

- ❏ 6-INCH GRAPEVINE WREATH
- ❏ ARTIFICIAL BERRIES
- ❏ ASSORTMENT OF NUTS
- ❏ PINECONES
- ❏ BEARDLESS WHEAT
- ❏ ARTIFICIAL RASPBERRIES & TINY GRAPES
- ❏ FALL LEAVES
- ❏ GLUE GUN & GLUE STICKS

## BEFORE YOU BEGIN

*Be sure to save all everlastings from previous projects to make quick and easy centerpieces. Decorating miniature wreaths is an ideal way to use leftover berries and flowers.*

### Proportion and Preparation

**It is important** that all materials match the proportion of the wreath base. Smaller wreaths are an ideal backdrop for smaller materials, such as berries, small fruits and nuts.

**Wheat stalks** and other natural grasses can be split to reduce their circumference. Examine the stalk or grass, noting the subtle shade and grain variations. With sharp scissors, cut along the grain so the stalk separates evenly (below).

**If certain materials,** including grasses and pinecones, seem too large, cut them down to scale. Work carefully so the materials do not break or fall apart when cut.

Grape clusters are made smaller by removing some of the peripheral grapes with scissors.

**Artificial berries** are often sold in clusters that may overwhelm a small wreath. Carefully pull off berries, one at a time, in the same way you would remove a leaf from a flower stem (below).

**Pinecones** are found in many sizes. To reduce a larger cone, simply cut through it, snipping the interior stem near the bottom so that the cone doesn't fall apart.

### Security's Sake

• To secure a nut with wire, push the wire end through a small hole drilled in the base, then wrap the extending wire around the wreath.
• To secure pinecones with wire, slip florist's wire into one of the lower layers. Bend the wire around the interior stem and twist the ends together, leaving them long. To wire cones into a cluster, twist the long wire ends together.

# MAKING A WREATH OF FRUIT AND NUTS

**HANDY HINTS**

**For holiday sparkle,** spray paint the nuts gold or silver several times, letting the paint dry between coats.

**To add glitter** to the fruit, spray paint only the tops with gold, then sprinkle sugar over the wet paint to create a frosted effect.

**Once the wreaths** are no longer needed as centerpieces, fix wire loops to the backs of the wreaths and hang them in a grouping on a bare wall.

1 Separate artificial berries into individual clusters of three berries. Glue berries around wreath in a circular pattern, with clusters evenly spaced and placed alternately on outside and inside edges.

2 Working with a selection of filberts, pecans, almonds and chestnuts, glue largest nuts onto wreath in three separate clusters, evenly spaced around wreath. Glue smaller nuts around each large nut cluster.

3 Trim stems off beardless wheat stalks. Weave and glue pieces of wheat around outer and inner edges of wreath in a circular pattern. Glue raspberries and grapes between nuts to add color and texture.

4 Fill in any remaining bare spots with small pinecones. For a finishing touch, glue two small fall leaves to opposite sides of wreath. Carefully trim leaves, following natural curve of wreath, to match scale of wreath. Use wreaths as a decorative base for candles, vases or bowls. Optional: Finish wreaths with a polyurethane spray to preserve the arrangement and add shine.

# A Container Garden of Succulents

*Exotic succulents are pretty, easy to grow and satisfying to give.*

## BEFORE YOU BEGIN

*Though succulents come in thousands of shapes, textures and sizes, there are basically three types: stem succulents, leafy succulents and root succulents.*

### Growing and Starting Succulents

**Most succulents are easy** to grow, merely requiring direct sunlight and watering in the spring and cooler temperatures and very little watering in the winter when they are dormant.

**Start your own** succulents from cuttings. Cut an off-shoot and let it sit for a day to form a callus on the stem before planting.

**When planning an** arrangement in a container, choose different compatible species, varying between flowering, leafy, erect and shorter succulents (below).

### Know Your Succulents

**African milkbush** is an upright, elegant-looking plant with purple highlights on its green leaves.

**Pearl echeveria,** or Texas rose, features low-growing rosettes with budded stems. Use as a filler.

**Sedum cauticolum** is a mix of grayish blue leaves edged with maroon and pale pink buds. Trail it over the bowl's edges.

**Panda bear plants** have silver, velvety leaves. Use as fillers for a full effect.

**For a special** display, use unusual shapes like baby toes, split rocks, tiger aloe and silver spring (bottom).

pearl echeveria

panda bear

African milkbush

sedum cauticolum

baby toes

split rocks

silver spring

tiger aloe

# PLANTING A GARDEN OF SUCCULENTS

**HANDY HINTS**

**Dust can sometimes** accumulate on the leaves of succulents, so be sure to wipe them occasionally with a damp, clean cloth. During the growing season, you can also spritz the leaves and stems lightly with water.

1 To determine placement, position plants as desired in a clay saucer, then remove plants and set aside. Fill the bottom of the saucer with a 2-inch-thick layer of clean gravel to provide proper drainage.

2 Prepare the soil base by mixing together two parts of sterile, purchased potting soil with one part of sand or vermiculite. Layer the soil base over the rocks until the saucer is two-thirds full.

3 Wearing gardening gloves to protect your hands, carefully remove the plants from their pots and place them so their roots sit directly on the soil. Position the plants close together, but avoid overcrowding.

**TAKE NOTE**

**The spines** on the stems and leaves of many cacti can be extremely painful and hard to remove. To prevent mishaps, always wear gloves when handling cacti.

**You can also fold** several pieces of paper together and then wrap and loop it around the cactus to make it easier to move.

4 Once the arrangement is in position, add another layer of soil to anchor the plants. Press the soil firmly against bottom of the saucer. To finish, cover the soil with a layer of decorative gravel, filling in the spaces between the plants.

# FLORAL DISPLAYS FOR CANDELABRAS

*Add flowers to a candelabra to create a stunning gift.*

## YOU WILL NEED

- ❏ CANDELABRA & CANDLES
- ❏ CHICKEN WIRE
- ❏ FLORIST'S FOAM
- ❏ FLORIST'S TAPE
- ❏ FLORIST'S SCISSORS
- ❏ IVY TRAILS
- ❏ ITALIAN PITTOSPORUM, LILY, SWEET WILLIAM, LISIANTHUS, QUEEN ANNE'S LACE

## BEFORE YOU BEGIN

*When decorating candelabras, consider all of the floral possibilities, as well as various arranging styles.*

### Long-Lasting Arrangements

**A chandelier candelabra** provides the perfect opportunity for a beautiful flower showpiece. To create a long-lasting arrangement, substitute fresh flowers with silk varieties.

**Begin by stringing** silk strands of ivy along the chain that attaches the chandelier candelabra to the ceiling. Allow the ivy to hang a little below the fixture.

**Then choose garlands** of silk flowers that match the style of your decor and wrap them around the candelabra. If necessary, use florist's wire to secure the garlands.

**With shorter strands** of ivy, fill in any empty spaces.

### Alternative Arrangements

**For an elegant affair,** decorate a candelabra with fresh flowers arranged in a horizontal manner.

**Cut pieces of florist's** foam to fit inside each candlestick, allowing the foam to be approximately 2 inches taller than the rims.

**Using florist's tape,** wrap the foam to the candelabra.

**Using ivy,** create the horizontal line of the arrangement, allowing pieces to trail gracefully.

**Arrange flowers** that create a formal feel, such as lisianthus, anemone and bluebell. Begin with shorter stems and build up to create a full shape without gaps.

# DECORATING A CANDELABRA WITH FLOWERS

**HANDY HINTS**

**If your floral display** is slated for one night of glory, then choose flowers that are fully conditioned and open when you arrange them. If you hope to enjoy them for an extended period, then start with flowers that are still closed.

1 Cut two 3- by 5-inch pieces of florist's foam; soak in tepid water. Cut two 4- by 6-inch sections of chicken wire; wrap around the soaked foam to keep the pieces from crumbling. Twist the wire ends to enclose the foam.

2 Hold the pieces of florist's foam in position on either side of the center of the candelabra. Using florist's tape, run a continuous wrap of tape repeatedly around the pieces until they are secured.

3 Poke lengths of ivy and pittosporum into the caged foam. Twine the ends of the greenery through the candelabra.

5 Insert white, no-drip candles in the candelabra. To prolong the freshness of the flowers, particularly the formal lily, keep the arrangement in a cool place until just before presenting the gift.

4 Insert the white lily into the caged florist's foam first. Follow with sprigs of royal purple lisianthus, magenta Sweet William and ivory-toned Queen Anne's lace. Aim for a balanced distribution of colors.

# NATURAL CLUSTER WREATH

*Tidy bunches of dried naturals make for a warm and welcoming wreath suitable as a gift for anyone's door.*

### YOU WILL NEED

❏ TWIG WREATH BASE
❏ WHEAT & SETARIA GRASSES
❏ LOTUS PODS
❏ TANSY & ACHILLEA
❏ SAFFLOWER
❏ AUTUMN LEAVES
❏ RAFFIA & FLORIST'S WIRE
❏ GLUE GUN & GLUE STICKS

## BEFORE YOU BEGIN

*When the stems of flowers or foliage are either too short or too fragile for use, hold their heads high on a wire stalk of your own making.*

### Wiring Plant Materials

**When securing** a heavy-headed flower to wreaths, make an artificial stem to strengthen it because a heavy head tends to droop under its own weight.

**Push a length** of florist's wire through the center of the flower head from below (right), extending it far enough so that about an inch of the wire protrudes above the blossom. Bend the tip over to form a hook.

**Gently draw the wire** back down until the hook is buried in the blossom. When the flower is fully dry, wrap the lower end of the wire around the dry stem and finish with florist's stem-wrap tape.

**To lengthen short stems,** cut off all but the top inch of the original stem. Place a wire alongside the remaining section as a splint. Starting from the top of stem, wrap a length of fine rose wire tightly in a spiral to join them.

**Continue winding** the rose wire (below) for 3 inches to hold the stem firmly in place; trim the excess. When using wired flowers in a wreath, be careful to hide wires.

### Heavy Heads

Among the prime candidates for wiring are the following flowers (below):

• Sunflower: disk-like in form with golden petals around the rim.
• Dahlia: distinguished for their open-centered but densely-folded, multicolored flowers.
• Zinnia: full blossoms 1 to 4 inches in many colors.
• Peony: red, pink, white and yellow cabbage heads that grow up to 6 inches across.

# MAKING A CLUSTER WREATH

**1** Construct several bunches of mixed dried flowers, much as you would assemble a bouquet. Arrange each group so that the blossoms nest comfortably. Trim the stems to make the bottoms even.

**2** Secure each bundle as you complete it by wrapping the stems with floral wire. Wrap them several times at a point roughly 10 inches from the top. Then wrap raffia around the stems to disguise the wire.

**3** Arrange the bunches of flowers on the wreath form until there is a satisfactory balance. Using a glue gun, fix the bunches in place. If they seem loose, secure them in place with wire, camouflaging the wire.

## HANDY HINTS

Before decorating a wreath, make some provision for hanging it, such as a sturdy wire loop on the back. Once decorated with fragile dried flowers, it will be awkward to turn the wreath over to work.

Dried seed pods, unusual materials to use in a wreath, can be very effective, as can various dried wild and ornamental grasses. Look for them in the fall growing in meadows, by the roadside or in the flower garden before end-of-season clean-up chores are done.

**4** Hot-glue a loose scattering of colorful fall leaves. Dried oak or maple leaves can be counted on to provide a particularly brilliant russet accent. As a finishing touch, make an informal bow, using multiple strands of natural-colored raffia, and attach it to the wreath.

# FRUITY FLORAL BOUQUETS

*Create a unique gift using fruit as a colorful, sturdy base for fresh flower arrangements.*

**YOU WILL NEED**
- ❑ CLEAR VASE
- ❑ LEMONS
- ❑ FORSYTHIA BRANCHES
- ❑ SCABIOSA
- ❑ AGAPANTHUS
- ❑ TULIP
- ❑ SOLIDAGO
- ❑ VARIOUS GREEN LEAVES

## BEFORE YOU BEGIN

*Choose bouquet combinations thoughtfully. The selected fruit should enhance the flowers on display, not overpower them.*

### The Aesthetics of Pairing Fruit and Flowers

**Before starting the** bouquet, consider color and scale when matching up fruits and flowers.

• Harmonious colors, such as the sunflower/kumquat duo (above left) are usually a safe bet.

• A monochromatic scheme (above center) works, as the deep hue of the cranberries reinforces the rose petal color.

• Analogous colors, as evidenced by the iris and limes

(above right) look a bit more dramatic. The built-up "wall" of limes mimics a vase within a vase.

• Since the flowers carry the most importance, make sure that the fruit is proportionate to the blooms displayed. Grapefruit or large apples, for example, would overwhelm freesia or other delicate flowers.

### Picking Fruit

**Fruit and flower** arrangements will be more successful with certain types of fruit.

**Leathery or thick-skinned** fruits hold up best under water. Good choices include lemons, limes, kumquats, sturdy apples or pears and firm grapes.

**Don't use delicate fruits** that would rot quickly and turn the water cloudy. Avoid most types of berries, bananas and Concord or other soft grapes.

# PAIRING FRUIT WITH FLOWERS IN A BOUQUET

**HANDY HINTS**

**Warm weather** yields gorgeous flowering shrubs that offer the wealth of a florist's shop in your own backyard.

**Try to pair up** fruit and flowers that will last about the same length of time to get the maximum mileage out of both.

1 Choose a large, clear container with an attractive shape. Add enough fresh, blemish-free lemons to fill the vase approximately up to the water fill line. Fill the container with fresh, cold water.

2 Cut the forsythia branches on an angle and remove flowers that will fall below the water line. Carefully position several forsythia branches in the vase to create the basic frame shape of the arrangement.

3 Add the secondary flowers—agapanthus and scabiosa—to the arrangement to reinforce the height and shape and introduce a pleasing color contrast. Add a variety of green leaves for additional filler.

4 Heighten the beauty of the arrangement with about eight tulip blooms of the palest yellow. The large blooms visually balance the weight of the lemons. Finish the arrangement by filling in any empty spaces with solidago.

# FLOWERS IN UNUSUAL CONTAINERS

*Add character to an arrangement with an unconventional container, and surprise a friend with a whimsical gift.*

### YOU WILL NEED
- ❏ CHILD'S WOODEN CHAIR
- ❏ CHICKEN WIRE
- ❏ GREEN SHEET MOSS
- ❏ FLORIST'S FOAM
- ❏ PITTOSPORUM, GALAX, SNAPDRAGON, DELPHINIUM, LILY, DIANTHUS & HEATHER
- ❏ STAPLER & CLIPPERS

## BEFORE YOU BEGIN

*Consider old toys, odd containers and jewelry boxes when looking for a fresh new way to display plants and flowers. Be sure to protect holders from the elements with waterproof liners.*

### Recycled Antiques

**An antique cigarette box** makes a shallow container for wild blue gentian, fresh cut from the meadow (right). Like most container adaptations, the shallow box needs a watertight liner to prevent leaking or rusting out the metal. Place a bud vase inside the container and fill it with water.

**An old-fashioned hat box** is a showpiece for Easter tulips (left). Plant bulbs in a pot filled with soil mix in the winter and store it in a cool, dark place. To force flowers in the spring, move the pot into the hat box, keeping the soil moist, and place the set in bright, indirect light.

**An antique toy wheelbarrow** holds an assortment of planted geraniums (right). The charming wheelbarrow disguises a standard window box that fits trimly inside.

### Chair Preparations

**The best choice** for the chair project at left is one that has lost its rattan center and has a ready-made opening. It is possible, however, to cut a hole in a solid seat if you have, and are handy with, a keyhole saw.

**Trace the circle,** then drill a starter hole just inside the circle large enough to insert the saw blade.

**Saw around the circle** with a keyhole saw, then sand and stain the chair.

# MAKING THE ARRANGMENT

**HANDY HINTS**

**When watering,** which should be done daily, put the container, chair and all, in a sink. Or, carry it outside, as the excess water will drip through the moss onto the surface below.

**Floral foam is** available in green foam for fresh arrangements or in gray or brown for dried arrangements.

1 Measure chicken wire 6 inches wider in all directions than chair's hole (Before you Begin); cut with clippers. Place wire on chair. Push down in middle of wire to form hollow and staple wire to underside of chair.

2 Fill bottom and sides of wire "nest" with moss, green side down. Cut piece of floral foam to fit in hole. Soak foam in water until heavy. Insert foam in center of moss nest and press down until secure.

3 Cut all stems on angle, then begin to shape flower arrangement, starting with pittosporum and galax leaf. Follow with taller stems including snapdragon, delphinium, lily and dianthus to define height.

4 Finally, fill in arrangement with heather to soften general look. Examine arrangement from all sides and fill in any empty areas. Fill arrangement enough to complement chair without overwhelming charm of chair.

**TAKE NOTE**

**Antique containers** can be expensive. But equally satisfying arrangements can be created using odds and ends rescued from a yard sale. It takes a good eye, some imagination and perhaps a coat of paint, but it's well worth the effort.

# FRAGRANT WREATHS

*Give the gift of fragrance for the nose and beauty for the eyes with this lush wreath of leaves and seeds.*

## BEFORE YOU BEGIN

*Many plants are known for their fragrances that live on long after the leaves and flowers have dried. Include one or more in your next wreath or bouquet.*

### The Fragrant Garden

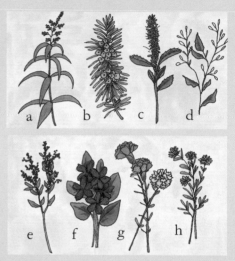

**Lemon verbena** (a) is a perennial shrub with masses of long-blooming pale purple or white flowers. It is named for its lemony scent.

**Rosemary** (b), a member of the mint family, has needle-like dark green leaves and typically pale blue flowers. It has a pleasantly spicy aroma, making it a favorite in the kitchen.

**Hyssop** (c) is a shrub that produces blue to purple flowers with a mild aroma of anise or licorice.

**Jasmine** (d) is a twining shrub whose white and pink varieties grow very fragrant flowers.

**Mimosa** (e) produces sweet-scented fuzzy, pinkish flowers and finely textured fern-like leaves.

**Sweet violet** (f), the most fragrant of the low-growing violets, produces an incomparably fragrant blue flower.

**Pink, or dianthus** (g), is notable for its typically clove-like, spicy fragrance and its pink to red colorations.

**Pennyroyal** (h) is of the mint family, with pinkish flowers and a minty tang to its leaves.

### Good Scents

In ancient times, it was widely believed that flower and leaf scents could cure many ills, including ills of the spirit. Some recommendations:
• Rosemary to preserve youthful vigor and strengthen memory.

• Sweet marjoram for those given to "much sighing."
• Basil to stimulate the heart and relieve melancholy.
• Sage and clary sage for soothing and calming.
• Cinnamon to alleviate exhaustion.

# MAKING A FRAGRANT WREATH

1 Using a pair of pruning shears, cut the large branches of seeded eucalyptus into smaller, 7- to 8-inch stems. In making the cuts, follow the natural branching pattern of the foliage for best effect.

2 Secure the end of the spool wire to the frame by twisting it around several times until firm. Holding two or three bunches of leaves at the same location, make tight turns of wire around the stems and frame.

3 Continue working in the same direction, adding overlapping bunches by binding with wire. Each succeeding group of bunches should cover the stem bases of the bunch before it and hide the wire.

## HANDY HINTS

**Eucalyptus** is known for its slightly pungent fragrance, but using large quantities of it can become overwhelming. Make certain to work in a well-ventilated room.

## TAKE NOTE

**There are a few** precautions that may help prevent allergic reactions when working with pollen plants. Try misting the plants or hairspraying the blossoms to keep the pollen from dispersing through the air as it is handled.

4 Complete the circle by tucking the final bunches of stems under the first bunches to form a seamless circle of foliage. Tie off the spool wire, then twist some wire to create a loop for hanging from the back. Straighten any twisted leaves or buried seeds.

# DRIED FLOWER COLLARS ON BASKETS

*A plain-looking basket accented with a collar of dried flowers makes a beautiful way to present a gift of any kind.*

## YOU WILL NEED

❑ 14-INCH BASKET
❑ GREEN SHEET MOSS
❑ DRIED FLOWERS
   INCLUDING LARKSPUR,
   YARROW, SUNFLOWER,
   POPPY SEED HEAD,
   TALLOW BERRY
   & CARTHAMUS
❑ GLUE GUN & GLUE
   STICKS
❑ FLORIST'S SCISSORS

## BEFORE YOU BEGIN

*Dried flowers can be chosen and arranged to create a variety of looks, ranging from a casual country feeling to a more elegant air.*

### Dried Flower Formality

**Almost any flower** can be dried, but to create a specific look, choose from the dried flowers shown in the chart (below).

**Dried flower arrangements** using grasses, herbs and seed heads have a casual and country feeling. In contrast, the addition of flowers such as rose and peony creates a more formal arrangement.

**Wildflowers found** along the side of a country road or in the woods are quite casual in appearance, as are many common garden flowers. They work well with dried grasses, herbs and seed heads.

Cultivated flowers, such as rose, delphinium and hydrangea tend to be more formal. Often it is the larger flower heads that command attention and add a touch of formality to the arrangement.

The coloration of the flowers also affects the formality of the arrangement. For instance, darker colored flowers, in shades of purple, burgundy and blue, look more formal than the sunny shades of yellow, orange and gold. Dark green foliage, such as eucalyptus, is more formal than goldenrod or wheat.

| Popular Dried Flowers | |
|---|---|
| **Formal** | **Informal** |
| Anemone (Windflowers) | Acroclinium (Sunrays) |
| Celosia (Cockscomb) | Amaranthus (Prince's Feather) |
| Digitalis (Foxglove) | Carthamus (Safflower) |
| Freesia | Chrysanthemum |
| Gladiolus | Helianthus (Sunflower) |
| Magnolia | Helichrysum (Strawflower) |
| Matthiola (Stock) | Tagetes (Marigold) |

### Containers

Containers are instrumental in setting the mood of an arrangement.
• Use containers that are rustic and simple in style to emphasize an informal arrangement. Woven baskets, terra-cotta pots,

stoneware and simple ceramics are ideal for a natural or country look.
• Formal arrangements call for more sophisticated containers made from china, glass, pewter, silver or copper.

# MAKING A DRIED FLOWER COLLAR

1 Wipe rim and surrounding area of basket clean. Tear sheet moss into small clumps and use glue gun to attach them around rim of basket. Drape sheet moss over edges to completely cover rim.

2 Always attach largest flowers first. With glue gun, attach sunflowers and then golden yarrow onto moss. Press flower gently to ensure it is glued to basket and not just moss. Continue around rim of basket.

3 Continue gluing smaller flowers, such as larkspur and carthamus, around edge. Space flowers in pleasing pattern. Fill in with poppy seed heads, firmly attaching them to basket and moss.

4 Accent flowers and seed heads with white tallow berries. Remove any visible strands of glue. Once glue has dried, fill the basket with a display of pinecones, potpourri or an arrangement of dried or fresh flowers. Since basket opening will be smaller once dried flowers are in place, choose an arrangement that is not so large or ungainly that it will harm or dislodge collar. If a section of collar is damaged, wait until display is in place and reattach or replace damaged flowers with new ones.

# MINI FLOWER TREE ARRANGEMENT

*Create a contemporary, tree-like gift with beautiful flowers.*

## BEFORE YOU BEGIN

*To make a mini tree arrangement with fresh flowers, select strong blooms with sturdy stems to support the flower heads. Fragile flowers, such as anemones, can be used as long as they are well conditioned.*

### Conditioning Flowers

**To help** the arrangement look its best, place fresh materials in water for a few hours before arranging them (right). This will help the arrangement last as long as possible.

**Even if** the stems have already been cut diagonally, recut them immediately before putting them into the arrangement.

**Remove all lower** leaves from the stems. This is especially important for a tree-like arrangement in which the stems are positioned to resemble a tree trunk. Even for traditional arrangements, it is important to remove any leaves that fall below the waterline to prevent rotting.

**Woody stems** benefit from having the bark scraped off the bottom 2 inches. After scraping, slit through the center of the stem 2 inches up from the base, then cut the slit stem diagonally, exposing the greatest amount of stem surface to water.

**Anemones are** fragile blossoms with a tendency to open quickly. To help prevent premature opening, keep the flowers stored in their cellophane wrapping and stand them in water, submerging three-fourths of the stem, in a cool room overnight. Prior to arranging them, cut the stems diagonally and place them in tepid water and floral preservative.

### Securing Stems

• Secure and hold the stems upright with a decorative ribbon or tie that complements and enhances the flowers and container.
• Fresh flowers look best when held in place with ribbon or lace.
• Dried flowers call for a more natural look. Bind their stems with paper ribbon or raffia.
• Even cellophane, with its vivid colorations, can be tied into an exquisite bow, giving the display a contemporary touch.

# MAKING THE MINI TREE ARRANGEMENT

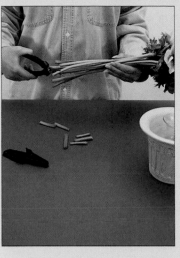

## HANDY HINTS

**When selecting** containers, make sure the neck of the glass jar or vase is wide enough to hold all the flowers, but narrow enough to help support the vertical position of the stems.

## TAKE NOTE

**To help extend** the longevity of a fresh flower arrangement and to keep flowers blooming, add fresh water to the vase daily.

1 Select an opaque container that is at least one-third the height of the flowers. Apply floral adhesive or double-sided tape to the bottom of a narrow-necked glass jar or vase to secure it inside the decorative container.

2 Arrange the flowers from the middle outward. Place each stem parallel to the preceding stem, keeping them straight and close together to form a "trunk." Make sure all the stems are the same length.

3 Wrap florist's wire around the center of the stems to secure them in a straight, vertical position. Place them in a jar filled with tepid water and floral preservative. Cover the wire with a ribbon bow.

4 Cover the inside of the decorative container with small patches of green sheet moss to hide the glass jar and provide a naturalistic base for the tree of flowers. Fill in the area between the container and the glass jar as needed to support the layer of moss. Leave a small, barely visible opening to make it easy to add fresh water.

# COLORFUL SAMPLER WREATH

*Group favorite flowers together for a gift that bursts with happy and festive color.*

## BEFORE YOU BEGIN

*Depending on the moisture content of your flowers, choose from two different drying techniques that preserve their colors, forms and brilliance.*

### Drying Fresh Flowers

**The best flowers to use** in dried arrangements are ones picked just before they reach full bloom. Otherwise, once dried, they become very fragile and tend to fall apart. Choose from one of two drying methods:

**Silica drying** is preferred when maintaining brilliant colors is desired. Silica gel is a sand-like substance whose crystals absorb moisture in the flowers. Lay flower heads faceup on a bed of silica, with more crystals sprinkled over to fully cover. Seal in an airtight box for about seven days. Flowers such as larkspur and rose benefit from silica drying.

**Hang-drying involves** natural air drying. It typically produces softer, more textured-looking materials. Remove the lower leaves from the stems and tie the flowers in small, loose bunches. Staggering the flower heads allows air to circulate between them. Hang the flowers upside down in a dry, cool, dimly lit place for a week or two. Flowers such as chrysanthemum, marigold and safflower are good candidates for air drying.

**Hang-dried flowers** need protection until ready to be used. Place individual stems in flexible straws and poke the straws into florist's foam (below).

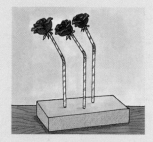

### Wreath Forms

Wreath foundations come in many materials. Essential characteristics are that they are lightweight and that they can be easily shaped into rigid circles.
• Twisted grapevine is a good choice for heavy fruits, cones and other large natural ornaments.
• Straw is ideal for lightweight flowers.
• Wire is traditional for large wreaths of branches such as fresh evergreens.

# MAKING A SAMPLER WREATH

1 Cut the dried flowers in 6- to 8-inch stem lengths and form each sample into five bundles, each secured with spool wire. You need enough of each kind to fill about one-fifth of the circumference.

2 Lay 25 flower bunches out in the rotational order you will use them. Wrap the free end of the spool wire around the wreath form and tie a tight loop. Leave the running wire attached to the spool to maintain tension as you add bunches of flowers.

3 Lay the first dried bundle on the wreath base with the stems following the curve. Secure the stem portion to the wreath with two wrappings of wire. Working in the same direction, lay additional bunches on the wreath and secure with wire. Be sure to maintain the spacing so there is a full sequence of five different bunches for each fifth of the wreath.

4 Continue adding bunches until the entire frame is covered. When you reach the last space, insert the stems under the adjoining bunch to hide them.

# GARDEN VEGETABLE VASES

*For delectable-looking gifts, try this novel variation on vases.*

## BEFORE YOU BEGIN

*Once the notion of wrapping containers in vegetables takes root in your imagination, many alternative designs will pop into mind.*

### Vegetable Variations

**Scoop out the center** of a perfect cabbage head and insert a can or plastic bowl. Hot-glue the inner leaves to conceal the liner and fill it with yellow roses (below left).

**Fix crisp leeks,** string beans or celery around a container and fill it with an abundance of bright red tulips or roses (below right). Wrap a raffia tie around it for a beautiful touch.

**Slice two firm** globe artichokes in half lengthwise. Hot-glue the artichokes, with the cut sides facing inward, onto the four moss-covered sides of a plastic food-storage container. Fill the can with brilliantly colored, short-stemmed poppies.

**Pluck out the center** of a coarse-textured, curly edged head of purple kale. Bury a container inside it. Fill the container with water and arrange fresh cut lavender and pink bachelor's buttons.

**Trace the outline** of a can or flower container on the top of a pumpkin and scoop out the insides. Fill the container with rusty orange or bright yellow chrysanthemums for a lively contrast of colors.

**Open the top** of a turban squash or a green buttercup squash and clean out the interior. Fill it with an arrangement of daisy-like helenium in shades of red and yellow. Or add sunflowers or black-eyed Susans—all late summer to fall blooms.

# MAKING VEGETABLE-WRAPPED VASES

### HANDY HINTS

**To ensure freshness,** make the vegetable-wrapped vases near party time and store them in the refrigerator until just before the guests arrive. Wrapping the containers in a damp dish towel will also help keep them fresh.

**If the labels** do not peel off easily from the cans, soak them in water until the glue has dissolved.

1 Strip the labels off a 13-oz. can, a 28-oz. can and a coffee can. Spray paint them green so they blend with the moss; let dry. Hot-glue sections of sheet moss to each, making sure to create an even surface.

2 Hot-glue each vegetable lengthwise to the moss, making sure the vegetables are positioned close together. If they reveal too much moss, alternate them to get a tighter fit, carrot top pointing up, then bottom up.

3 Measure and cut several generous lengths of raffia, gather the strands and wrap them firmly around the carrots, covering the can, finishing with a pretty bow. Repeat for all the other vegetable-covered cans.

4 Fill the vegetable-wrapped vases two-thirds full with water. Arrange bouquets of fresh snapdragons, using a different color for each. Snapdragons make excellent cutting flowers and come in white, lavender, pink, rose, yellow, orange and red.

# SHAPED WREATH

*Anyone will appreciate the creativity of a uniquely shaped wreath.*

## BEFORE YOU BEGIN

*Making an interesting shape for the foundation of a wreath ensures a unique display piece.*

### Basic Choices

**The basis of** all wreath making is a sturdy frame.

**Floral supply shops** and hobby shops often carry a variety of ready-made circular shapes in materials ranging from twisted grapevine to wire and plump straw. They come in single or double rings.

**These prepared bases** are also commonly available in a choice of diameter sizes, from 8 or 10 inches across to diameters up to 36 inches.

**When it comes** to irregular shapes like stars, rectangles and hearts, try creating your own wreath foundation.

**It is possible** to make forms freehand, but for added strength you can employ the technique shown below, using common materials found around your house.

**Assemble the following:** heavy-gauge wire, a sheet of plywood, a hammer, 10 nails, a pencil and a ruler.

### Make Your Own Base

• To make a star-shaped base, begin by drawing a five-pointed star, working either freehand or with a ruler to guide you, on a piece of plywood (below). The star pattern should measure between 10 and 18 inches from point to point.

• Drive a nail at each peak and valley of the star. Wrap an end of the wire around the top nail (below) and continue bending the wire around successive nails until the figure is complete. Twist the wire ends together at the top.

# MAKING A STAR-SHAPED WREATH

1 To make the star freehand, bend sections of the heavy wire, taking care to make each section the same length. When you return to the starting point, overlap the two wire ends and secure them with spool wire.

2 Build up the wreath form by adding clumps of Spanish moss, attaching them to the base with turns of spool wire as you go. The moss will give the frame bulk and provide an anchor for the flowers.

3 Begin wiring on the smaller plant materials, starting with alternating clumps of alchemilla, larkspur, salvia and amaranthus. Use a continuous length of the small-gauge spool wire and wrap as you proceed.

4 Use a glue gun to attach the larger flower heads— yarrow, field sunflower, celosia, peony, marigold and button mum—onto the built-up base. Vary the flower colors and shapes for a beautiful display.

5 Complete the star-shaped wreath by securing a pretty bow with hot glue. Given the country-style informality of the wreath, a bow fashioned from several loops of raffia is particularly attractive.

# THE LANGUAGE OF FLOWERS

*Send a sentimental message using the age-old symbolism of flowers.*

## YOU WILL NEED

- ❏ WINDOW BOX
- ❏ PLASTIC LANDSCAPE CLOTH
- ❏ COARSE GRAVEL
- ❏ POTTING SOIL
- ❏ POTTED GERANIUM
- ❏ POTTED IVY
- ❏ GREEN SHEET MOSS

## BEFORE YOU BEGIN

*Give a floral arrangement extra-special purpose by choosing flowers not only for their beauty, but for their meaning.*

### Flowers and their Meanings

**In the Victorian era,** the language of flowers was a means of communication widely used in polite society.

**Meaning was attached** to hundreds of flower species and translations were generally known or else required the services of a floral dictionary.

**Use the flower symbols** (below) as a guide to arranging flowers with special meaning for an everyday display or for a specific occasion.

**For an everyday** arrangement in your home, display red geraniums (comfort) and ivy (friendship) in a window box. Fill in empty spaces with green moss (maternal love).

**For a going-away party,** join sweet basil (good wishes), a sprig of spruce (farewell) and forget-me-not (true love).

**For a Fourth of July** celebration, combine nasturtium (patriotism) and oak leaves (courage).

| Glossary of Floral Symbolism | |
|---|---|
| **Flower Name** | **Meaning** |
| Amaryllis | Pride |
| Aster | Love |
| Camellia | Loveliness |
| Carnation, red | Aching heart |
| Cornflower | Delicacy |
| Daffodil | Chivalry |
| Forget-me-not | True love |
| Gardenia | Secret love |
| Gentian | Injustice |
| Gloxinia | Sudden love |
| Honeysuckle | Sweetness |
| Jasmine, yellow | Elegance |
| Lily | Purity |
| Lily-of-the-valley | Return of happiness |
| Magnolia | Dignity |
| Orange blossom | Innocence |
| Pansy | Remembrance |
| Peony | Bashfulness |
| Primrose | Youth |
| Snowdrop | Renewal |
| Violet | Modesty |
| Wallflower | Faithful |
| Water lily | Pure heart |
| Wisteria | Friendship |

# ARRANGING A MESSAGE OF COMFORT

**HANDY HINTS**

To ensure that your message is enjoyed for its meaning, include a note. Describe the arrangement's symbols and the source of this charming tradition.

1 Line the inside of your container with plastic landscaping cloth. Alternatively, use an oversized, heavy-duty trash and leaf bag. Overlap the corners to prevent water leaking out.

2 Fill the bottom of the container with a layer of coarse gravel for drainage. Cover the gravel with a layer of potting soil mix to a depth sufficient to permit the growing plants to take root and prosper.

3 Remove the geraniums and ivy (Before you Begin) from their pots and arrange them inside the container, giving each space to fill out without being crowded. Allow the ivy to hang over the sides of the container.

4 Use additional potting soil to fill the planter, and tamp the earth to firm the arrangement. Tuck a layer of sheet moss (Before you Begin) around the edges to retain moisture and nutrients. Water and feed the plants as recommended.

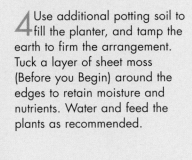

# PEPPER BERRY ARRANGEMENTS

*These colorful, aromatic, long-lasting displays make exciting gifts and spice up any decor.*

## YOU WILL NEED

- ❑ TWIG WREATH FORM
- ❑ STALKS OF PINK PEPPER BERRIES
- ❑ PROTEA PODS
- ❑ GREEN & BURGUNDY AMARANTHUS
- ❑ PINK LARKSPUR
- ❑ BAY LEAVES
- ❑ GLUE GUN & GLUE STICKS

## BEFORE YOU BEGIN

*Worth their weight in gold in ancient times, the fruits of the Piper nigrum vine are as decorative as they are tasty.*

### The Romance of Pepper Berries

Ever since Alexander the Great invaded India in 327 B.C.E. and discovered the pungent, bead-like fruit of the pepper vine, this Asian spice has been highly valued in the West. Explorers, including Columbus, risked everything to keep it in steady supply, and in the process stumbled on the New World. The search later fueled centuries of colonial warfare in the tropical regions of the world.

**The berries that** inspired these deeds grow on broad-leafed vines widely cultivated on the Asian subcontinent, in the West Indies and in tropical South America.

**The pepper vines** bear green berries on slender flower spikes. Those berries destined to become commercial spices are harvested before ripening and then dried until the flesh of the seed coating becomes wrinkled and darkens to the familiar blackish brown of black pepper. White pepper comes from the same source, only it is the pepper seed without its outer covering.

**Ornamental pepper berries** are also taken from the Piper nigrum vine, but are used only after the fruits have been allowed to ripen to the pink or red colors (below) so valued in display arrangements.

**Stalks of pepper berries** intended for use in craft arrangements must be handled with particular care because the berries are attached by the slenderest of stems. The leaves that come with the berries do not dry well and are usually removed.

### Alternatives

A multitude of other natural materials can be added to embellish the wreath, including:
- Dried pomegranates, gourds, mini pumpkins, nuts and other small types of fruit.
- Plump, papery seed heads of poppy and nigella pods.
- Dried mushrooms, fungi, pinecones and chile peppers.
- Holly with berries and snowberries.
- Starfish, seashells and other seashore artifacts.

# ARRANGING A PEPPER BERRY WREATH

1 Lay the twig wreath base on a flat surface. Using the glue gun, hot-glue alternating spikes of pink larkspur, green and burgundy amaranthus in a spiral pattern, following the lay of the foundation wreath.

2 Hot-glue a half dozen plump clusters of dried protea to the wreath, spacing them at roughly equal intervals around the circumference. Bury the woody stems in the twigs so only the clusters show.

3 Attach large clumps of the reddish pepper berries to the wreath, again following the spiral lay of the twigs and the other dried materials. Handle the berry clumps with particular care or they will shed.

## HANDY HINTS

Create a miniature spice bush with leftover pepperberries. Mix plaster of paris in the plastic liner of a terra-cotta pot. Insert a curly willow stick upright in the center and allow to dry overnight.

Pierce a plastic foam ball and secure it atop the stick. Attach green sheet moss to the ball with florist's wire. Hot-glue clumps of pink pepper berries over the entire surface of the mossy ball (the thicker the better). Place additional green moss around the base of the stick to simulate ground cover.

4 Accent the wreath with dried bay leaves around the inner circle of the frame. Add the leaves one at a time, inserting them with their stems inward along the red pepper stalks as though they were pepper "leaves." The result will be both colorful and aromatic.

## TAKE NOTE

Wreaths made with any sort of dried plant materials are bound to be fragile. To keep handling to a minimum, place the twig wreath base in the chosen location before adding berry and floral stalks. Position the hanging nail in the wall and attach the wire loop at the back of the wreath. This way, the wreath can be hung immediately when done.

# FRUIT-AND-FLOWER CENTERPIECE

*Dress up a table with a unique display of fresh flowers and fruits, then send the creation home with a lucky guest.*

## YOU WILL NEED
- ❏ FLORIST'S FOAM
- ❏ BASKET & PLASTIC LINER
- ❏ FLORIST'S PICKS
- ❏ GALOX & LEMON LEAVES
- ❏ QUEEN ANNE'S LACE
- ❏ SUNFLOWER
- ❏ HYDRANGEA
- ❏ GRAPES & PEARS
- ❏ RED & GREEN APPLES
- ❏ GRANULATED SUGAR
- ❏ FLORIST'S SCISSORS

## BEFORE YOU BEGIN

*Sugar-coated fruit is very simple to create and adds sophisticated sparkle to a floral centerpiece on an elegant dinner table.*

### Frosting and Wiring Fruit

**Sugar-frosted fruit** is for decoration only. It could cause food poisoning if eaten.

**Separate three eggs.** Put the egg whites into a small bowl and use a whisk (hand or electric) to beat them until fluffy but still liquid.

**Use a pastry brush** (below) to coat each piece of fruit completely with the egg whites.

**Working over a** large plate, sift or sprinkle granulated sugar over the covered fruit (below). Small fruit can be rolled in sugar, though this may cause lumping.

**Let sugar-frosted** fruit set on a flat surface for thirty minutes before inserting it into the arrangement.

**Small clusters** of fruit such as grapes and cherries should be wired to a florist's pick (below) to strengthen and lengthen the stems before inserting them into the florist's foam. It may be easier to do this before frosting the fruit.

**Insert toothpicks** into small single fruits such as strawberries or kiwis so they can be firmly positioned in the arrangement.

**For large, heavy fruits** such as apples and pears, insert florist's picks directly into the fruit.

# MAKING A FRUIT AND FLOWER CENTERPIECE

## HANDY HINTS

**If the flowers** start to wilt, refresh them by recutting the end of each stem at a sharp angle. Immediately reinsert into well-watered foam.

**For a quick** alternative to egg whites, spray the fruit with lemon juice and then sprinkle with granulated sugar.

1 Soak a block of florist's foam in water for several hours. Measure the plastic basket liner and cut the foam to fit, leaving enough room around the edges to add water. Put the liner and foam into the basket.

2 Use a sharp knife or florist's scissors to recut the stems of the galox and lemon leaves. Insert the stems all around the upper outside edges of the foam to form a base for the flowers and fruit.

3 Wire small clusters of grapes to florist's picks and insert the picks directly into the bottoms of the apples and pears. Coat the fruit with granulated sugar and allow to dry (Before you Begin).

4 Use the florist's picks to insert the fruit into the top and sides of the foam, leaving adequate room for the flowers. Position the grapes so that several clusters drape elegantly over the sides of the basket.

5 Recut the flower stems at an angle. Wire any floppy stems to florist's picks. Insert the larger flowers, such as sunflower and hydrangea, into the arrangement. Fill in spaces with Queen Anne's lace.

# GIFTS OF
# ACCENTS &
# ACCESSORIES

*Gifts for the home are always suitable. Don't worry too much about entirely matching a place's decorating scheme. These ideas are designed to accent and accessorize ... not take over or build an entire theme. Here you'll find pillows, plaques, rugs, placemats, towels and so much more ... all related to the home, all easy to make, and all beautiful. With so many ideas here, you'll wonder where to start ... and you'll probably find some ideas to treat yourself (and your own home) with!*

# AROMATIC PILLOWS

*Add a pretty scent to pillows to create a cherished gift.*

## YOU WILL NEED

- ❑ ¾ YARD FABRIC
- ❑ ⅜ YARD COORDINATING FABRIC
- ❑ 1⅜ YARDS WELTING
- ❑ ⅜ YARD TULLE
- ❑ 12- BY 12-INCH PILLOW FORM
- ❑ POTPOURRI
- ❑ NEEDLE & THREAD
- ❑ SEWING MACHINE & ZIPPER FOOT

## BEFORE YOU BEGIN

Add pockets of potpourri to a pillow insert for a scented pillow or sachet.

### Preparation

• Cut 13- by 13-inch squares: two from pillow fabric, one from tulle, one from lining.
• Cut ruffle strips: two strips 7 by 45 inches from pillow fabric; two strips 5 by 45 inches from coordinating fabric.
• Place potpourri in sealed plastic and crush large pieces with a rolling pin (below).

### Pocket Plan

**Mark lining square** to form pockets for potpourri. Divide piece into nine equal squares. Label each square 1 through 9 and each marking line A, B, C and D as indicated.

```
        A           B
    ┌───┊───────┊───┐
    │ 7 │   8   │ 9 │
    │   ┊       ┊   │ ····· D
    │ 4 │   5   │ 6 │
    │   ┊       ┊   │ ····· C
    │ 1 │   2   │ 3 │
    └───┊───────┊───┘
```

# Making an Aromatic Pillow

**1** Pin welting to right side of pillow square; allow ½-inch seam allowance. Clip corners of welting and overlap welting at meeting point. Stitch welting to pillow front using zipper foot.

**2** For ruffles, sew short ends of strips, right sides facing, to form continuous strips. Fold strips in half lengthwise, wrong sides together; press. Mark strips into four equal sections.

**3** Sew gathering stitches along unfinished edge of strips. Gather strips so markings line up with pillow corners. With a zipper foot, stitch inner ruffle to right side of pillow front.

**4** Pin outer ruffle to right side of pillow cover, above first ruffle. Stitch, using zipper foot. Welting should remain visible on right side. Allow extra fabric at corners so ruffle lies flat.

**5** Stitch tulle to marked lining around sides and bottom edge. Stitch down lines marked A and B. Insert equal amounts of potpourri into sections 1, 2 and 3. Stitch along line C. Insert potpourri into sections 4, 5 and 6.

**6** Stitch along line D. Insert potpourri into sections 7, 8 and 9, filling all sections evenly. Sew along top edge of lining to complete potpourri pillow insert. Shake piece gently to distribute potpourri evenly.

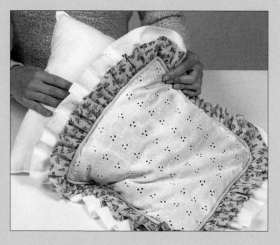

**8** Clip corners and grade seam allowances. Turn pillow cover right side out. Steam out any wrinkles. Insert pillow form into bottom opening. Fold in seam allowances and hand-stitch bottom edge closed.

**7** Hand baste tulle side of pillow insert to wrong side of pillow front. With right sides together, use zipper foot to sew pillow front to pillow back. Leave large opening along bottom edge to insert pillow.

# POTPOURRI DOOR SACHET

*This small, aromatic sachet makes an elegant gift.*

### YOU WILL NEED

- ❏ EMBROIDERED SILK FABRIC
- ❏ ½-INCH-WIDE DECORATIVE RIBBON
- ❏ ¼-INCH-WIDE SATIN RIBBON
- ❏ HEM TAPE
- ❏ POTPOURRI
- ❏ BROWN PAPER
- ❏ SCISSORS

## BEFORE YOU BEGIN

*Use bits of fabric, a snip of ribbon and some sweet-smelling potpourri to create a beautiful, cone-shaped sachet to hang on a doorknob in any room.*

### Using the Template

Enlarge the template (right) on a photocopier to desired size. Or transfer it to graph paper and then enlarge it to the desired door sachet size.
• To make the cone pattern, trace the enlarged template onto brown paper and cut out.
• Enlarge the template at different percentages to make an assortment of various-sized sachets.

• Place the arrow along the fabric grainline for cutting.

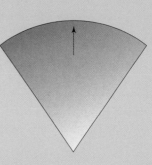

### Making Potpourri

Collect sweet-smelling flowers and herbs from your spring or summer garden. Some favorite scents are: rose, carnation, geranium, honeysuckle, lilac, lavender, rosemary and mint.

After the flowers and herbs are cut, spread the petals on absorbent paper and place them in a warm spot, but not in direct sunlight. Allow enough time for the petals to dry—about four to five days. The petals will shrink as they dry, so be sure to collect and dry enough to fill the cone.

Prepare the potpourri mixture by layering the petals in a jar and sprinkling them with salt and an orrisroot

mixture: use 1 ounce orrisroot, 1 ounce brown sugar and 1 ounce of powdered spices to 1 quart of dried petals.

Add spices like allspice, clove, cinnamon or nutmeg. Bits of dried lemon rind, orange rind or rose oil will also lend a fresh aroma.

Continue layering the petals and spices until the jar is full. Gently and thoroughly mix the layers, then cover the jar. Allow the mixture to age for three weeks, stirring it twice weekly to blend.

Pack the potpourri petals lightly into the sachet.

# MAKING A POTPOURRI DOOR SACHET

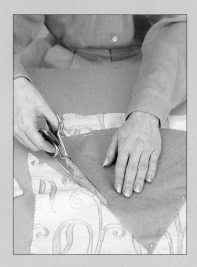

**HANDY HINTS**

On very fine or loosely woven fabric, it may be necessary to increase the seam allowance, stitch the seam twice or use a zigzag stitch to keep the fabric from unraveling.

**QUICK FIX**

As the scent diminishes from the potpourri, untie the ribbon and refill the cone with fresh potpourri or add scented oils.

1 Lay the embroidered silk fabric right side up on the work surface. Pin the brown paper pattern (Before you Begin) to the fabric. Using scissors, cut out the potpourri cone following the template's edge.

2 Press the hem tape in half lengthwise. Insert the upper raw edge of the fabric into the hem tape fold; pin in place. Carefully stitch through all layers of the tape and fabric, encasing the edge.

3 Right sides together, fold the fabric in half, matching the top edge and forming a cone. Stitch a ¼-inch side seam. Press the seam open halfway down; avoid creasing the sides.

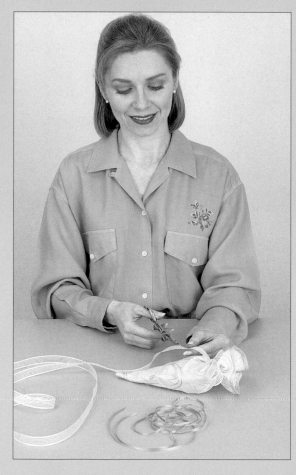

5 Gather the top edge of the cone together and tie a decorative ribbon bow around it, 1½ to 2 inches from the top edge. Using scissors, trim the ends of the bow so they are even. Hand stitch an 8-inch loop of ¼-inch satin ribbon to the back of the cone at the seamline to hang around the doorknob.

4 Turn the cone right side out. Fill up to 2 inches from the top with potpourri (Before you Begin). Gently shake the cone while pouring to allow the mixture to fill the bottom.

# HOUSE PLAQUES WITH DISTINCTION

*Personalize this welcoming gift with the recipient's family name.*

## BEFORE YOU BEGIN

*The family name will be there for all to see when it's glued to a plaque and positioned by the front door.*

### Selecting Materials

• Decide on the wording or numbers and select a style. Arts and crafts stores and some hardware stores carry these supplies.
• The plaque itself can be wood, marble, slate, cast-iron, glazed pottery or a small slab of stone.
• Choose a plaque and letters that suit the character of the family as well as the style of the house.

• Colorful, plastic stick-on decals are also available at arts and crafts stores and come in both floral and geometric patterns.
• Select transfers small enough to fit comfortably within the spaces left after the letters are placed.
• If the plaque is not wood but the letters are, protect everything, including the decals.

### Choosing Alternatives

**Plaques can also act** as signs and include both the family name and address. A short family name looks best on a vertical sign (right).

**Try a red cedar plaque** with black letters, white with all lowercase letters or black with chrome letters.

**Put longer** names on horizontal signs. Or combine "the" with a shorter name to fill out the top line (below).

# DECORATING THE PLAQUE

1 Lightly sand the letters and numbers. Sand the surface and edges of the plaque, removing any burrs or rough areas. Take care not to sand away the ridges of the molding edge.

2 Place the plaque on a flat work surface and prime the front and back. Let dry. Then apply two coats of one of the colors of paint, allowing paint to dry between coats.

3 Place the letters on the work surface and prime the fronts. Prime the backs as long as they have no adhesive. Let dry. Paint with two coats of the darker color. Let paint dry between coats.

4 Position letters and all the decals on the plaque and adjust all the elements until they look balanced. With a pencil, lightly mark position of the letters and decals on tops and bottoms.

5 Apply a thin layer of wood glue to the backs of the letters and position them on the plaque where they were planned in pencil. Let them dry for at least an hour.

6 Trim away any white edges on decals for a clean look. Then peel off the backs and reposition the decals on the plaque where they were planned.

7 To make the plaque weatherproof, apply two coats of polyurethane varnish or a clear acrylic seal. Allow each coat to dry overnight or according to the manufacturer's recommendations.

# COLOR-WASHED BASKETS

*Enhance the natural appeal of wicker with a soft color wash that matches your friend's decor.*

## BEFORE YOU BEGIN

*Washing is a simple technique of adding water to paint to dilute it. The effect of washing creates a soft, matte finish.*

### Preparing the Paint

**A wash finish** will reveal the natural wood grain and tone of the basket through the paint.

**Before painting,** dilute some flat latex paint with water (below); one part paint to four parts water. Latex paint is ideal for wood surfaces because it's easy to use and dries quickly. Premixed paints for colorwashing are also available at many painting and craft stores.

**The color** of the original wood surface will influence the finished look of the wash: the lighter the wood, the lighter the wash will be. Although pale washes work best on light wood surfaces, they can be applied to dark woods after a simple priming step.

**Lighten dark wood** by first whitewashing the surface. When it is dry, wash the basket in the desired color. For a layered look, wash the basket with different colors. Allow each layer to dry for 10 minutes, then rub down (below) to remove some of the paint.

### Basket Prep

Most wooden-slatted baskets have a varnish that must be removed before beginning the colorwashing process.
• Remove any dirt or grease with a sponge or soft cloth and mild, soapy water.

Rinse with clear water and allow the basket to dry.
• With sandpaper, lightly sand the surface to remove the varnish gloss, then wipe it clean with a lint-free cloth.

# APPLYING A COLOR WASH FINISH

1 Cover the work surface with brown paper or newspaper. Slightly roughen the basket surface with a medium-grade sandpaper so the paint will adhere better. With a soft cloth, remove all dust from sanding.

2 Using a sponge brush, apply water-thinned latex paint (Before you Begin) to the outside of the basket. Be sure to paint with the grain and in even strokes. Allow the basket to dry for 5 to 10 minutes.

3 With a lint-free cloth, wipe or rub the painted surface to remove some of the paint, creating a washed effect on the wood. If a darker look is desired, apply a second coat of paint and repeat the rub-down process.

## HANDY HINTS

**Colorwashing** can be applied to any wooden surface. It's as easy to colorwash furniture and cabinets as it is small items like baskets.

## TAKE NOTE

**Remember to** sand and wipe the basket clean between coats of paint or sealer. This process will allow the next coat of paint to adhere better to the surface of the basket.

4 Allow the basket to dry completely. Lightly sand the surface again and remove the dust with a soft cloth. Coat the basket with one or two coats of acrylic sealer. The sealer can be applied with a sponge brush or sprayed directly onto the basket surface.

# PAINTED WOODEN PLACE MATS

*Folk art wooden place mats will add color and character to any table setting.*

## BEFORE YOU BEGIN

*For the place mat base, find a sheet of chipboard at a local craft store or lumberyard.*

### Preparing the Chipboard

Select a ⅜-inch-thick chipboard that is large enough for four place mats, at least 48 by 60 inches.
• With chalk, mark four 12- by 15-inch rectangles on chipboard. Mark in 2 inches from each corner. Connect marks to edges, creating diagonal corners.
• Cut out with handsaw, taking care not to split diagonal corners. Gently sand edges with fine-grade sandpaper until smooth.

### Planning the Design

**On prepared chipboard,** measure in 3 inches from all four edges and mark, creating rectangular area for center checkerboard design.

**On oaktag,** draw rectangle in same dimensions as rectangle on chipboard.

**For checkerboard** pattern, draw vertical and horizontal lines that are 1 inch apart within oaktag rectangle.

**To create checkerboard** stencil, cut out every other square in every other row.

**On a photocopier,** enlarge design templates (below) and trace each design onto oaktag for border stencils. Carefully cut out each design.

# MAKING A WOODEN PLACE MAT

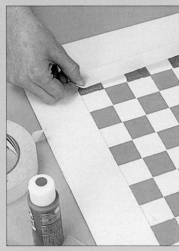

**HANDY HINTS**

Cookie cutters are great sources for stencil designs. Outline the cookie cutter on oaktag and cut out.

**TAKE NOTE**

To avoid smearing, remember to let the paint dry before moving on to the next stencil.

1 Sand edges of chipboard pieces (Before you Begin) until smooth, being careful not to distort corners. Cover both sides of each piece with white paint. Once dry, gently sand any rough spots; apply second coat.

2 Align checkerboard stencil on marks (Before you Begin); secure with tape. With sponge brush, paint squares blue; let dry. Move stencil one square down and one square over; secure. Paint squares blue; let dry.

3 For painting border, apply masking tape to outer edge of checkerboard, to keep edges straight and even. Apply one or two coats of green paint to outer edge, creating a solid-colored border on place mat.

4 Starting at corners, position bird stencil (Before you Begin) on green border. Paint red with sponge brush. When dry, stencil and paint each animal from templates. Continue around place mat, letting each stenciled animal dry before painting next design.

5 Carefully peel back masking tape once paint is thoroughly dry. Apply polyurethane sealer to each place mat, front and back, to waterproof. Allow first coat to dry before applying second coat of sealer.

# WRAP-AND-TIE PILLOWS

*Create a unique gift with the simple twist of a scarf around a pillow.*

## BEFORE YOU BEGIN

*Tie silk scarves, bandannas or fabric around existing pillows for a quick and refreshing change.*

### Scarf Selection

**Scarves and bandannas** are excellent choices for wrap-and-tie pillows. They are available in a wide range of patterns, colors and sizes, plus the edges are finished.

**When selecting scarves,** keep in mind the size of the pillow and the number of scarves that will be needed.

If the pillow will be wrapped in a single large scarf, the scarf should be at least two-and-a-half times the measurement of the pillow. If a pillow will be inserted between two scarves, the scarves should be at least 8 to 10 inches larger than the pillow.

### Tying Alternatives

**To tie corner knots,** hold the scarf ends together and wrap them around two fingers to form a loop. Insert scarf ends through the loop and pull tight (below).

**To create rosettes,** secure all four scarf corners together with a rubber band. Fold the tip of each end and tuck them under the rubber band; fluff (above).

### Wrap and Tie

Fabric yardage may be used to wrap the pillow.
• Select a fabric that drapes easily like challis, gauze and soft cotton.
• Avoid stiff fabrics such as heavyweight linens and sailcloth.

• Choose a washable fabric for easy cleaning.
• To prevent raveling, finish fabric edges using pinking shears, a zigzag stitch or a narrow hem.

# MAKING A SCARF PILLOW

**HANDY HINTS**

Apply a stain-resistant spray to the scarves before making pillows.

1 With wrong side up, spread a large silk scarf out on a table. Position the pillow form on the scarf so that the scarf design is centered and the scarf corners are centered in the middle of pillow sides.

2 Starting at the opposite corners, pull the corners of the scarf together and wrap them with a rubber band. Pull the remaining corners of the pillow together, securing in the same rubber band.

3 Tuck in the scarf edges along the diagonals so the pillow form does not show through. Arrange the gathers evenly around the rubber band. Center the scarf design evenly on the front and back of the pillow.

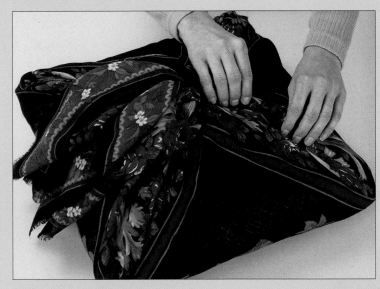

4 Fold three of the scarf tails back into the rubber band so the tails don't show. Cover all tails with the remaining tail, forming a small, puff-like shape. Tuck the edges around the rubber band so it does not show. Smooth the scarf across the pillow form.

# DECORATIVE STAMPED DESIGNS ON FABRIC

*Give any fabric gift a boost with paint, stamps and designs from nature.*

## BEFORE YOU BEGIN

*Give fabrics instant flair with stamps made from inexpensive foam sheeting. Achieve beautiful effects using a mixture of paint colors on some of the stamps.*

### Making a Stamp

**Use the leaf design** below as a template for the stamp. Trace it onto thin cardboard and then cut it out. To obtain different-sized leaves, enlarge or reduce the leaf on a photocopier.

**To make the stamp**, place the leaf template on the foam sheet and trace around it. Use a mat knife to cut out the design (below).

**Foam sheeting** is available in craft stores. It is a thin layer of smooth foam that is very easy to cut, making it perfect for stamp designs with detailed edges. It prints a more solid image than a sponge stamp.

**Cut a wooden block** ½ inch wider and longer than the foam stamp. Glue the foam to the block (below).

### Stamping Technique

• Before stamping an expensive home furnishing, practice on fabric scraps to get the technique just right.
• Place a scrap of fabric over a layer of plastic.
• Pour each fabric paint color into a separate small plastic container.

• Apply paint evenly to the stamp with a small foam brush.
• Lightly press the stamp onto the fabric and lift straight off.

## YOU WILL NEED

❏ Fabric
❏ Foam sheet & wood block
❏ Acrylic paint & plastic containers
❏ Wood glue
❏ Foam brush
❏ Scissors
❏ Mat knife
❏ Corrugated cardboard sheets

# STAMPING A PILLOW COVER

**1** Using a seam ripper, remove the stitches from one side of the pillow; remove the pillow form from the cover. Cut a piece of cardboard to fit snugly inside the pillow cover; insert it into the cover.

**2** Use a foam brush to apply paint evenly to the foam stamp; do not overload the brush. Be careful that paint does not drip onto the wooden block. Do not dip the foam stamp into the paint.

**3** Carefully place the stamp paint side down in the desired position on the pillow cover. Press it in place lightly but firmly with the palm of the hand. Carefully lift the stamp off the fabric without shifting it.

## HANDY HINTS

**To avoid mistakes** and an overworked design, plan the positions of the stamps carefully before starting to work. Mark the desired locations with an air- or water-soluble pen.

## OOPS

**Incorporate any drips** or smudges into the design. For smudged images, outline the motif with a darker color. To camouflage drips, add a few freehand squiggles or swirls in strategic locations to make the whole thing look like an intentional design.

**4** Apply more paint to the stamp each time you use it. Stamp all images in one color before changing to the next. Wash and dry the stamp between colors. For a two-tone effect, paint the inside of the stamp with one color and the outer edge with another.

# PAINTED DAMASK

*For a pretty gift, hand paint delicate woven designs on damask.*

## BEFORE YOU BEGIN

*Painting designs on damask is a sophisticated version of paint-by-number. Simply follow the woven designs to create luxurious handcrafted linens.*

### Damask-Painting Basics

Because the designs are already woven into the fabric, the biggest concern with painting damask is correctly mixing the paint and applying it to the item.

• Work under bright light so that the designs in the damask are clearly visible (top right).
• Mix one part paint with five parts water.
• Dip the brush into the paint solution, then dab the tip of the brush onto a paper towel to remove excess paint (lower right).

• Since the colors will migrate across the grain of the fabric, begin painting in the center of the design.
• To fill in the design, lightly brush the paint onto the floating threads of the fabric.

### Shopping for Damask

**Almost every** fabric store will carry damask fabric, but be aware that thick cotton damask with a large satin design is the easiest to work with. Intricate designs can sometimes present a challenge to paint.

**For premade linens,** scout department stores, yard sales and flea markets. If you find a nice piece of damask with a stain or flaw, either dye the damask to hide the stain or cut the good portion of the damask into napkins and place mats.

**Look for** yarn-dyed damask as an interesting alternative to plain white.

# PAINTING DAMASK

1 Cover a flat surface with paper to protect the area, then place a napkin in the center of the paper. Begin painting at one corner of the design and continue around the napkin with the same color paint.

2 Allow the first color to dry completely before adding the second color. Use a clean brush for each color. If possible, keep different colors from overlapping to ensure that the paint doesn't run.

3 Continue adding additional colors to the design until the desired effect is achieved. To avoid drips and spills, be sure to keep the bowl of paint close to the area being painted. Let dry completely.

4 When the design is dry, spray with a stain-resistant coating. To make a pillow, cut one piece of cotton the same width and ¾ the length of the napkin, and another piece the same width and half the length.

5 Along one edge of the width of a back piece, fold the raw edge under ¼ inch and press. Fold again ¼ inch and stitch along inner fold. Repeat for other back piece. The stitched edges will overlap on the pillow.

6 With right sides facing and raw edges aligned so that the back pieces overlap, pin and machine stitch back of pillow to damask front. Trim seams and clip corners; turn right side out. Press flat; then insert a pillow form.

# PIERCED PAPER LAMP SHADE

*Light shines through this pretty lamp shade for a special effect—a perfect gift for a special occasion.*

## BEFORE YOU BEGIN

*To make a new lamp shade, just remove the old shade and use it as a pattern piece.*

### Cutting Out the Shade

**To make a pattern** for the shade, open the old shade along its seam. Measure across widest point and from highest to lowest points. Use these sizes to determine how large a piece of paper to buy. Tape the old shade to the new paper. Outline the old shade with a pencil; then cut out the new one.

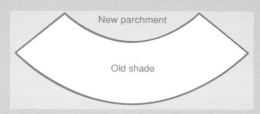

### Creating the Design

**Use the letters** below as templates for the words on the shade.
- Enlarge the letters to the right size on a photocopier and then trace them onto paper to create the phrase. Use this paper as a pattern for piercing.
- If preferred, use a different style of lettering. Remember that typefaces without much detail are easiest to pierce and to read.

**Trace the outlines** below onto paper to use them as patterns for the stars and moons on the shade. Use a photocopier to enlarge or reduce the patterns as desired. Plan the positions of the stars and moons carefully before starting to pierce.

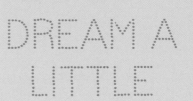

DREAM A
LITTLE

### Just a Phrase

Choose the words for the shade to suit the rest of the design and the room in which the lamp will stand.
- For a child's lamp shade, choose a phrase from a favorite fairy tale, nursery rhyme or lullaby.

- For a more grown-up shade, select a line from a favorite book or poem. Quotation books are often good sources of inspiration.
- Make sure the letters are large enough for easy reading on the shade.

# MAKING THE SHADE

### HANDY HINTS

**Parchment paper** is available from craft stores. Measure the dimensions of the old shade before buying, to make sure the sheet of parchment is big enough.

**Add interesting** texture to the lamp shade by using handmade paper or rice paper instead of parchment.

### TAKE NOTE

**Always use** a low-wattage bulb with a paper shade. Make sure the bulb does not touch the inside of the shade.

**1** Wrap parchment paper around small ring of old lamp shade. Using a glue gun, glue ring inside top edge of shade. Hold shade in place with clothespins until glue dries.

**2** Glue large ring close to bottom edge of shade, as shown in Step 1. Glue the vertical seam closed. Hold rings and shade together with clothespins until glue dries.

 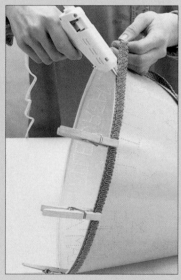

**3** Position the words pattern around the bottom of the shade. Hold in place with clothespins. Use a craft needle to pierce through the pattern onto the shade. Repeat with the patterns for the stars and moon. Make sure all the pierced holes are evenly spaced but not too close together.

**4** Glue the trim around the top and bottom edges of the shade ending at shade seam. Turn under the trim edge and glue in place. Pin the trim in place until the glue has dried.

# PATCHWORK PILLOW

*This pillow uses a traditional patchwork design with contemporary fabrics for a stylized look. Your friends will treasure this handmade gift.*

## YOU WILL NEED

❑ FABRIC
❑ PIPING CORD
❑ SHEETING
❑ PILLOW FORM
❑ SEWING MACHINE
❑ THREAD
❑ NEEDLE & PINS
❑ TAILOR'S CHALK
❑ RULER
❑ FABRIC SHEARS
❑ IRON & IRONING BOARD

## BEFORE YOU BEGIN

*Create this log cabin patchwork design on a square of sheeting to ensure a nice shape on the finished square.*

### Choosing the Fabrics

Carefully coordinated fabrics create a dramatic effect.
• Be sure fabrics are the same weight and composition.
• Use washable fabrics. Preshrink, if necessary.

• For a 15-inch-square pillow form, you will need ½ yard of mixed pale fabrics and ½ yard of mixed dark fabrics for patchwork, plus a 16-inch square for back of cover.

### Building Up the Blocks

**Cut a square of sheeting** 1 inch larger all the way around than the pillow form. Fold in half diagonally, and then in half again. Press, then open out. This creates a guide for the patchwork placement. Center first square, aligning corners with fold lines (right).

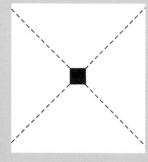

**The log cabin patchwork** effect is achieved by adding progressively longer blocks of fabric in a circular pattern. To get the pale/dark divide, work two pale blocks, then two dark blocks in rotation. The diagram (right) shows which order to place them in.

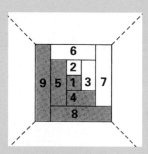

**The final square** should look like the example (right). This patchwork pillow cover is made from one large square, but you can join smaller squares—made from narrower patchwork strips—in groups of four or nine to get a more detailed pattern.

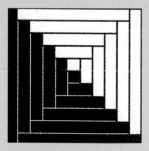

# MAKING A PATCHWORK PILLOW COVER

1 For a 15-inch pillow form, cut sheeting 17 inches square. Cut center for patchwork 1½ inches square, then cut patchwork strips 1½ inches wide. Do not trim to length—do this as you go along. Baste center square in position.

2 Take the first (pale) strip and lay along one edge of the center square, with raw edges matching and right sides together. Machine stitch down side to lower edge of center square, ¼ inch in from raw edge.

3 Trim off long end of strip to form a square level with the central one. Press strip open. Position second pale strip along the length of both squares and stitch, as before. Trim new strip to length and press open.

4 Repeat the process, alternating two dark strips with two light strips. Always work in the same direction around the block. Keep the seams exactly ¼ inch wide and press after stitching each seam.

5 To avoid wasting fabric, trim each strip to length after stitching it in place. Continue until patchwork strips are near the edge of the sheeting. Trim away surplus sheeting to make a 16-inch square.

6 Position covered piping cord around patchwork block, with raw edges matching. Stitch in place. Cut a piece of backing fabric 16 inches square. Right sides together, place backing over patchwork cover so cording is sandwiched between them. Stitch a ½-inch seam, leaving an opening in one side. Turn right side out, insert pillow form, and slipstitch opening closed.

# DECORATIVE TRIM FOR TOWELS

*These designer bath towels created with luxurious fabrics and trim make a great housewarming gift!*

## YOU WILL NEED

- ❑ BATH TOWELS
- ❑ ASSORTED TRIMS & FRINGES
- ❑ SEWING MACHINE
- ❑ MATCHING THREAD
- ❑ MEASURING TAPE
- ❑ SCISSORS & PINS
- ❑ IRON

## BEFORE YOU BEGIN

*Embellishing towels and linens with ready-made trims is one of the easiest and least expensive ways to refresh your decor.*

### Tips for Trimming Towels

**Trims are most effective** when placed widthwise (right). Trims stitched lengthwise are not fully visible when draped over a towel bar and fringe will fall at an angle instead of hanging straight.

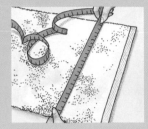

**Decorative towels can still** be functional if the trim is positioned at only one end. The untrimmed end can be used for drying hands.

**When trimming along the** towel bottom, place the trim parallel to the edge. For an overhang, position the trim or lace so that the top edge of the trim is ¼ to ½ inch from the bottom edge.

**Add ½ inch** to the width of the trim measurement for the side seams. Turn the trim under ¼ inch on each side to prevent the raw edges from raveling.

**Heavy trims and braids** will lie flatter against a towel than lightweight trims.

**Prewash trims so they won't** shrink or fade when washed.

### Design Ideas

Consider these creative ideas when embellishing towels and linens.
• Stitch a band of heavy lace across the bottom of a towel, then cut away the towel from behind the lace (below).

• Complement your decor by using upholstery and trim scraps as trimmings.
• For added decoration, stitch buttons, beads and trinkets on top of towel trimmings.

# TRIMMING A TOWEL

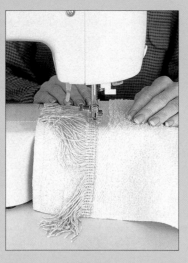

## HANDY HINTS

**Avoid washing towels** frequently to keep the trims from showing wear. Use lavish trims on decorative towels and add simple, less ornate trimmings to everyday towels.

**Spray fancy trims** with fabric protector to keep them from becoming stained.

1 Lay the towel, right side up, on a flat surface. Position the trim and fringe on top of the towel. Using sharp scissors, cut the fringe and trim ½-inch wider than the width of the towel; press the towel, fringe and trim flat.

2 Position the fringe so that the bottom of the fringe is even with the bottom of the towel. Turn the raw side edges under and pin in place. Machine stitch along the top and side edges of the fringe.

3 Position the trim on top of the towel so that the bottom of the trim overlaps the top of the fringe. Turn the raw side edges under and pin in place. Machine stitch along the bottom edge of the trim.

## DOLLAR SENSE

**Look for remnants** or discontinued trims in 1-yard pieces to save money on trimming towels. Another economical idea is to use trims cut from clothing or old linens.

4 Machine stitch along the top and side edges of the trim, being sure to catch the trim's raw edges in the side seams. Remove the pins and press flat with a warm iron. Comb through the fringe with your fingers to straighten it.

# Painted Borders on Fabric

*Perk up a plain pillow with a painted decorative border for an economical gift that looks fun and pretty.*

## BEFORE YOU BEGIN

*All you need is ½ yard of plain cotton fabric to create a simple flanged-edge sham to decorate with a fun, painted border.*

### Making a Pillow Sham and Design Templates

• From the plain cotton fabric, cut one 16-inch square for the pillow front plus one 16- by 13-inch rectangle and one 16- by 10½-inch rectangle for the pillow back.
• Press a ½-inch double hem across the width of each back panel.
• With the right sides facing and the raw edges aligned, position the two back panels on top of the front panel. Overlap the two back pieces so that their combined depth equals that of the front panel.
• Pin all the panels together; then machine stitch the seam ½ inch in from the raw edges.
• Trim each corner diagonally and press the seams open. Turn the pillow cover right side out.
• Topstitch around the cover, 2 inches in from the outer edge, to create a flange.
• Enlarge or reduce the bell and shell templates (below) to the desired size on a photocopier.
• Trace the templates onto stiff cardboard and cut out.

### Inspired Design

Nursery rhymes and fairy tales are great sources of inspiration for border designs.
• For a nursery rhyme alternative, paint a cow, moon, dish and spoon onto the border and then add the well-known accompanying words.

• Fun fairy tales to illustrate include Goldilocks and the Three Bears and Little Red Riding Hood.
• If you feel uneasy painting the words, omit them and just paint pictures all around the border.

# PAINTING A BORDER ON FABRIC

1 Lay pillow sham on flat surface. Using pencil and templates, transfer bell and shell patterns to pillow. Position shell and two bells in one corner and one bell in opposite corner.

2 Using gray paint, paint outline of each bell, then fill in center. Carefully paint around the top curve. When dry, use the brush to paint white details onto each bell.

4 When bells and shell are dry, use light pink paint pen to write words around border. Using paint pens, randomly add small colored dots around words and motifs. Let dry completely.

3 Outline shell with light lavender paint; then fill in center. When dry, begin layering pastel paints on shell; let each color dry before adding next. Using antique white paint, paint narrow horizontal bands along bottom and middle of shell. Using light pink paint, paint thin vertical lines on top of shell.

# PAINTED COTTON RUG

*This rug will warm any space with its colorful, geometric designs.*

## BEFORE YOU BEGIN

*Transform a plain, inexpensive cotton rug by painting large geometric shapes in vivid hues.*

### Preparation

Solid cotton rugs are available in many sizes and a variety of textures. Choose a woven pattern that is fairly flat and does not interfere with the overall design.
• Launder the rug first to remove sizing or extra dye from the manufacturing.
• Experiment with types of brushes. Bristle brushes, rather than foam brushes, are the most suitable. Square-cut brushes allow you to paint straight lines and precision corners without having to use a drafting tape. They also allow paint to be applied thickly, which is ideal for textured surfaces.
• The softer the rug, the more paint will be absorbed into it. To get a smoother surface and to conserve paint, first spray a washable acrylic paint over the entire top surface of the rug to serve as a background color.

### Painting Preparation

**Inspiration for eye-catching** geometric designs can be found in modern art books and profiles of contemporary architecture, in painting and decorative art museums, in your children's personal artwork, in the room's wallpaper or on upholstery fabrics.
**Experiment with shapes** and colors to create a bold design or simply adapt the pattern used here (below).

**Plan the rug's design** on a sheet of graph paper first. Draw the design to scale in a pleasing pattern or cut out paper shapes to arrange on the paper. For the most impact, keep the design large-scaled and use a maximum of three paint colors.

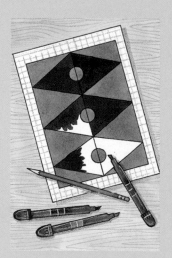

# PAINTING A COTTON RUG

**1** Follow the scaled drawing (Before you Begin). With a long straightedge and regular lead pencil, draw the complete design on the face of the cotton rug. Use a mechanical compass or template for circles.

**2** Apply 1-inch-wide masking tape to the rug along the outside edges of the pattern for the first paint color. For arcs, bend the tape around the outer curve, clipping it to lie flat along the inner curve.

**3** Allow the first coat to dry. Paint all sections of one color at one time before moving on to the next color. Tape off the areas for the second color, and paint these sections at the same time.

## HANDY HINTS

**Paint both sides** of a rug with the same or a different design. When one side begins to look "tired," turn the rug over for a fresh, new look.

**When working with** a heavily textured rug, use a stencil brush to work the paint into the fibers.

## QUICK FIX

**To prevent the** rug from slipping and bunching, place it over a nonskid, very thin rug pad made especially for rugs.

**4** Smaller areas, such as circles, are easier to paint freehand than by taping off because the previous painting establishes the circle boundary lines. For a neat edge, use a $3/8$- to $1/2$-inch-wide, square-tip brush.

**5** Paint the fringed ends using a tray or bowl of thinned paint and a bristle brush. Allow the fringe to dry on newsprint. Protect and seal the finished cotton rug with a water-repellent or waterproof stain-resistant spray.

# DECORATIVE BALLS

*These creatively decorated balls make a great hostess gift.*

**YOU WILL NEED**

❏ 4-INCH FOAM BALLS
❏ RAW PUMPKIN SEEDS OR OTHER DECORATIONS
❏ CRAFT GLUE
❏ PENCIL
❏ AWL OR KNITTING NEEDLE

## BEFORE YOU BEGIN

*Design clusters of decorated foam balls in a variety of colors and textures from everyday materials such as pushpins, thumbtacks, small grommets or even rope and twine.*

### Designing Decorative Balls

**Even the most** ordinary objects can be used to embellish foam balls. Found at craft stores, the inexpensive foam balls are available in 2- to 6-inch sizes.

**Let your imagination** govern the style of the ball. Look around the house for inspiration. For instance, sequins, rubber bands, pearls and pushpins are all interesting design materials.

**To create an Art Deco look** (right), simply cover balls with silver thumbtacks. Or spray twine-covered balls with glossy black enamel or shiny silver paint.

**For a "country"** feel, wrap three different sizes of balls with twine, string or layers of rubber bands. Place these simple, homespun spheres in a basket to complete the gift.

### Assembly Tips

Some materials may require special care for a perfect finish.
• Tiny or odd-shaped embellishments like corn kernels and shelled sunflower seeds are best sprinkled on.

• First, spread a thin layer of glue all over the ball. Then sprinkle on the seeds while holding the ball over a bowl (below left). If necessary, fill in any spaces by hand.
• If the materials selected will not overlap or abut completely, spray paint the balls before covering them. Match or contrast the paint color with the material to hide or reveal any empty spaces.

# MAKING DECORATIVE BALLS

1 To make a handle to hold while decorating, punch a hole with an awl or knitting needle into one side of a 4-inch foam ball and insert a pencil. A thin paintbrush handle or chopstick will also work well.

2 Holding the ball in one hand, squeeze out a half-dollar-sized circle of craft glue onto the side of the ball opposite the side with the handle. Place one raw pumpkin seed in the center of the glue circle.

3 With your fingers, place one seed at a time around the center seed. Place each seed in the same direction, with the small, pointed end toward the center seed. Allow the glue to dry before adding the next row.

4 Squeeze a narrow line of glue around the ball below the first row of seeds. Continue to position seeds, with the small, pointed ends toward center, in a circular manner, overlapping the seeds to keep the pattern consistent. Let dry between rows to prevent slippage.

# ORIGINAL MOSAIC ACCENTS

*Make unique gifts by applying mosaics creatively.*

## YOU WILL NEED

❑ Wide wood frame
❑ Glazed ceramic tiles
❑ Hammer
❑ Tile nippers
❑ PVA adhesive
❑ Mosaic grout
❑ Putty knife
❑ Sponge
❑ Stiff-bristle brush
❑ Acrylic sealer

## BEFORE YOU BEGIN

*When collecting materials to make mosaics, look for appealing colors and patterns, whether they come from fine china or broken tub tiles.*

### Simply Smashing Ideas

The beauty of this **ancient** and decorative art form is that you can use just about any rigid material that captures your fancy.

**Mosaics can be made up** of all manner of firm, small-scaled materials such as commercially available, precut ceramic and glass tesserae or seashells.

**Wall and floor tiles** are larger and provide greater pattern and texture variety. You can pick up damaged tiles inexpensively at a wholesale tile supply store, but even perfect tiles in small quantities fit a small budget.

**Or collect the pieces** from chipped or broken china and pottery that are beyond repair. This way, you don't have to throw away a favorite, sentimental dish.

**To make mosaic bits** of a broken plate or other clay material, wrap the object in a dish towel and tap it with a hammer (above). The idea is to crack, not shatter, the object into usable fragments, so use a light touch and check your work to be sure you don't break it into pieces too small to work with.

**Once the tiles are broken** into pieces, use tile nippers to shape the tiles into interesting pieces. Tile nippers are blunt-headed pliers used to remove curved sections on tiles.

### Painting Preparation

Many dull surfaces lend themselves to mosaics. The main criterion is that the surfaces be fairly rigid; a backing that flexes will eventually crack the grout. Consider the following:

• Insets in tabletops, such as coffee tables and counters.
• Metal cans, such as a watering can.
• Picture frames.
• Vases and boxes.
• Hurricane lamps.

# Adding Mosaics to a Frame

1 Gather enough tiles of uniform thickness and in various colors to cover a frame. Break them into pieces, then use tile nippers to shape the fragments to fit the frame and design (Before you Begin).

2 Starting in the corners, glue the right-angled pieces to the frame with PVA adhesive and a putty knife. Using a dab of glue on both the frame and tile bit, apply one piece at a time until the frame is covered.

3 After the glue sets, mix up the grout to fill the spaces between the tiles. Using a putty knife or spatula, spread the grout generously. When the grout is almost dry, sponge the tiles (but not the spaces) clean.

4 Allow the frame to dry for at least 24 hours. To protect the grouted spaces between the tiles from discoloration, brush on a coat of acrylic sealer. Or apply a washable paint to the grout lines for color. The paint will be absorbed into the grout, but the dried paint can be wiped off of the glazed tiles. Hang the frame securely, using an anchor suitable for the frame weight and wall.

# DECORATIVE SERVING TRAYS

*Add pretty papers to turn a plain tray into something special. Make an entire gift set if you wish!*

# BEFORE YOU BEGIN

*Paint adds an extra-summery touch to the tray's wooden trim. Choose a paint that complements the colors of the tissue paper.*

## Preparing the Tray

- If the tray is made of unfinished wood, it must be sanded with fine sandpaper before painting; remove dust with a damp cloth.
- Seal sanded wood with white primer. Let dry thoroughly. If wood has a glossy finish, choose a primer specially designed to adhere to glossy surfaces.
- Place masking tape around the inside edges of the bottom of the tray. Paint the sides of the tray with an acrylic paint. An extra coat of paint may be necessary, depending on the wood. Let dry; remove tape.

## Template Notes

**Use the templates** below to make it easier to create the painted designs. Enlarge the templates to the size you want on a photocopier. Rub pencil lead onto the back of the paper to cover the outline of the design. After gluing the tissue paper onto the tray, place design pencil-side down on the tray. Pressing down with a ball-point pen, draw over design outline to transfer it to the surface of the tray.

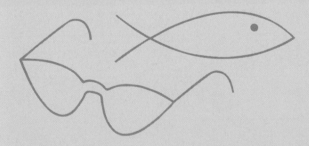

## Which Glue?

Spray adhesive is best for this job, but there are alternatives:
- Decoupage glue allows paper to be moved around. It works best with sturdy papers, but it may cause tissue paper to rip or run.
- Fabric glue is less expensive and easier to obtain than decoupage glue. It works the same way as decoupage glue.
- Both glues brush on white but dry clear.

# DECORATING THE TRAY

## HANDY HINTS

**This technique is** an easy way to revive an old, discarded tray. Almost any paper will do, including children's artwork or leftover wrapping paper. Paint the tray in bright, coordinating colors.

## OOPS

**If the tissue paper** tears, just place another piece on top of it.

**If the glue causes** the tissue paper colors to run on a glossy finish, wipe them up with a damp cloth. If colors run on a latex finish, let dry and then paint over them.

1 Tear several colors of tissue paper into different shapes. Arrange on tray with largest pieces underneath and smaller ones overlapping on top. Align straight edges of paper with sides of tray.

2 Remove paper from tray. Starting with larger pieces, spray wrong side with spray adhesive and apply to tray. Gently smooth out wrinkles with foam paintbrush. Continue with remaining pieces; let dry.

3 When tissue paper is completely dry, use a thin brush and acrylic paint to make bold, summery shapes such as sunglasses, sunshine, waves and fish on tray. Let dry completely before sealing.

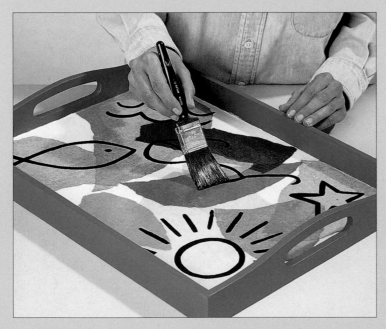

4 Seal entire surface of tray, including design area and painted wood, with two layers of polyurethane to prevent water penetration. Brush it on carefully to avoid ripping tissue paper. Allow each coat to dry completely. Do not sand in between coats.

# INDEX